From the
of the
River Severn

or

Florrie at Sallow Pier:

a season and life
supporting
Shrewsbury Town FC

Alan Manford

Published by:
Alan Manford, 1 Parkside Road, Handsworth Wood, Birmingham B20 1EL
almanford@yahoo.com

ISBN 0 9532726 2 1

British Library Cataloguing in Publication Data:
a catalogue record for this book is available from the British Library.

Design & production:
Country Books, Courtyard Cottage, Little Longstone, Bakewell, Derbyshire DE45 1NN

Printed & bound by:
Antony Rowe Ltd, Eastbourne

Acknowledgements:

Several people have contributed a lot of their time and energy to this book. My grateful thanks go to Lucy Harrison (for the illustrations) and to Amarjeet Sagoo (for the caricature of Arthur Rowley). I am greatly indebted to Mrs Joan Rowley and the late Arthur Rowley, Steve Ogrizovic and Tommy Lynch for being so generous with their time in granting me interviews. Peter Dolby also gave liberally of his time and I am deeply obliged to him for all his kind help. Thanks to Judy Shone for putting me in contact with Peter Dolby. Many thanks to Dale Kramer and Frank Manford for their witty contributions; and to the latter, along with Tyrone Marshall, for reading and commenting on draft versions. My love and thanks to Penny for her tolerance.

Dedicated to the memory of George Arthur Rowley.

View from half-way up the hill

"If history is going to repeat itself I should think we can expect the same thing again." – Terry Venables

I live half-way up a hill in Birmingham (which is perhaps better than at the bottom of a mine in Hungary, if Tibor Fischer is to be believed). If I stand at my bedroom window I can see the floodlights at Villa Park and marvel at the profligacy shown by a Premiership side that can afford to leave lights on long after the game has finished. When I'm in my garden and the wind is in the wrong direction I can hear the crowd baying at the Hawthorns, home of West Bromwich Albion. I drive twenty minutes to my work at a school in Small Heath. From there I can see Birmingham City's St Andrews stadium – little more than the distance of a throw by Thomas Nielson or David Hughes (who, for the sake of the uninitiated, are two players in the recent history of Shrewsbury Town who were capable of particularly long and useful throw-ins). If I catch the train from the station at the foot of the hill, it's a seven minute journey to the station that serves Walsall's Bescot Stadium (or the "Biscuit Tin" as it is affectionately known to rival fans with an ear for a pun and an eye for a metaphor).

So, given the proximity of all this allegedly higher grade football, why do I dedicate one Saturday in two during the months from August to May to driving a round trip of almost a hundred miles, sitting in a car for one and a half hours in each direction? This is a question that directly or indirectly might be answered somewhere in the course of these pages.

I haven't always lived half-way up a hill, of course – that's part of it. I was brought up on the North Shropshire Plain – a case of Cold Hatton Heath rather than Small Heath. There football clubs were much thinner on the ground; then, as now, there was only one Football League team in Shropshire. Moreover in those days it is possible that the fortune of local clubs counted for more, in that youngsters were not subjected to non-stop televised football and brainwashed into desiring brand-names and replica versions of the kit worn for part of a season by Premiership teams. Nowadays by the time a boy (or girl, for that matter) is ten he will undoubtedly have seen Manchester United play more times than his nearest local team, even if his father does take him to some football matches.

As well as being brought up in North Shropshire, I was also born and lived the first seven years of my life on Shrewsbury Street in the Shropshire village of Prees (as pictured below). The street name was possibly of some subliminal significance, as was Shrewsbury Town entering the Football League in August 1950 at roughly the same time that I was beginning to show some awareness of the world.

A few words from the Manager (with apologies to Paul Whitehouse – and Kevin Ratcliffe)
"No-one hands you cups on a plate." – Terry McDermott

....Shrewsbury Town. Erm? Football. Ah. Isn't it... you know... The smell of Bovril. Thwack of leather on leather. Coracles in the Severn. Coracles on the pitch. Squelch of mud. Balls hoofed over the stand into the river. Arthur Rowley in baggy shorts. Marvellous. Isn't it? Pipe-smoke drifting across the terraces. Leaves scattering over the stand and across the pitch. Ducks, geese, pigeons flying over in ones and twos, or in formation.... Arthur Rowley in baggy shorts.... Cold concrete terrace beneath the feet. Drumming on corrugated sheeting. Catch us if you can, eh, coming down the Wyle Cop? Glimpse of the Abbey.... Glimpse of the Castle.... Steam trains slowing as they pass behind the stand. From the banks of the River Severn.... Oh, blue and amber! Amber and blue!...

Thursday 19th July, 2001
"Merseyside derbies usually last ninety minutes and I'm sure today's won't be any different." – Trevor Brooking

Bridgnorth Town (away); Shropshire Senior Challenge Cup
5-0 (HT 3-0); Freestone (17, 31), Jemson (32), Rioch (69), Lowe (80)
Attendance: 210
Standpoint: Sitting fairly close to the half-way line.

The game had a warm, friendly atmosphere partly generated perhaps because there is no history of rivalry between the two clubs (indeed there is precious little history of any games between them), and the few spectators that were there were interested in football rather than delighting in its attendant ills. Most of the crowd seemed to be supporters of Shrewsbury and I suspect that many Bridgnorth fans were either also Shrewsbury fans or at least did not mind too much losing to the county's only League team.

The other main factor in the cosy atmosphere was the stadium itself, from the on-site bar with pool-table, to the refreshingly amateur tea-hut (not only non-commercial in its prices, but run by a delightfully obliging lady who made me a replacement cup of tea because of my fastidiousness over the amount of milk I take), and the intimate ground. This intimacy comes mainly through the closeness of the spectators to the pitch and the fact that the noise of the crowd is quiet enough not only for spectators to hear the words of wisdom passed between players and what the referee is saying to control the game, but also, should the people wish, to join in. The intimacy is also engendered by the size of the stadium and the way it is hemmed in so tightly on two sides by houses. So close are the houses that when the ball was kicked into the garden of the same bungalow twice within five minutes it was rather like little boys having to ask for their ball back from the neighbours.

One example of the referee's verbal control that I heard was him telling Leon Drysdale and a Bridgnorth player to "watch your elbows or I'll have you both". He did not have too difficult a job in respect to monitoring violent play because, although there were some hard tackles, it was generally a sporting game. There was also one instance that might be classified as control exerted by the crowd, when the Bridgnorth centre-half was admonished for his overly aggressive intent; the look on his face was one of sheepishness verging on chagrin.

The bloke next to me remarked, "What does Mark Atkins make of this? A couple of years ago he was with Blackburn."

"Pretty much the same as Nigel Jemson might," I replied.

The game at this level is littered with players who have known better days, who have paraded their skills in crowded arenas, who have been valued at more than would pay for the entire outfit that they have now fallen in with. For whatever reason (whether the early promise was never realised, the ability reduced by injury or time) they find themselves surplus to requirement at the highest level, but at least they are still playing football and Third Division football does pay some bills.

"You'd think that the time Nigel Jemson has been in the game he'd have learnt to dive more convincingly."

"Maybe; but he's still one of the best passers of a ball that's been at Salop for several years."

The pitch at Crown Meadow has a slope that would have rivalled the legendary pitch at Yeovil's Huish (sadly replaced by a new out-of-town ground in 1990, and now a Tesco supermarket, presumably with trolleys specially adapted to compensate for the incline). On this evening Crown Meadow also had long grass and an apparently uneven surface. As the ball went into touch because Steve Jagielka had failed to control it, someone enquired, "Trouble with the boots, Jags?"

"Yes, I've got 'em on the wrong feet, I think," he replied with admirable self-deprecation.

"You're not used to playing on a ploughed field," someone commented, presumably trying to be nice to Mr Jagielka, but being very uncharitable towards his hosts.

The queue to the tea-hut at half time was so slow moving that people were swapping life stories, falling in love, making their wills, phoning their mothers, arranging mortgages, completing Open University degrees, filing for that divorce they'd put off for so long.... Chick Bates strolled past. Chick (or "Philip" to his mum) had a couple of spells as a player with Salop and managed them for a while during their heady days in the old Second Division. He has been in management at one or two other clubs (including being assistant manager at Celtic, I vaguely remember), but is now Head of Youth Strategy, or something equally nebulous, at Salop. "Hi, Lennie," he said to someone in the group behind me. I was impressed that someone should be on first name terms with Chick Bates.

Half a minute later another passer-by made the same greeting.

After a few more moments the penny dropped. I realised to whom they were talking. This was not someone who had been christened Leonard, this was none other than *the* Lennie, Lennie the Lion, the Shrewsbury Town mascot. He was not so easy to spot out of his cat-suit, but the scantly bearded figure was of the right stature – small, slight of frame, low centre of gravity, full of restless energy, moving with the same gait as when impersonating a cuddly toy.

Lennie's group was joined by a young man with a digital camera. "I asked Gregor [Greg Rioch] if I could take his picture. Matt Redmile went past at that moment and said I'd need a wide angle lens for that."

"He's a good one to talk."

Their conversation, apart from the question of who owed whom five pounds, was mainly about the New Meadow and particularly the attitudes of Sutton Farm residents living near the proposed site. When and where Shrewsbury Town get a new stadium is a topic set to recur throughout a million Salopian conversations for a long time yet. The young man with the digital camera said he had a letter published in a local paper (and might therefore have been one R.Oldacre, whose letter arguing the need for a new home for Shrewsbury Town and urging people to vote in the referendum on the matter appeared in the *Shropshire Star* on Wednesday, July 18th).

It was good to see Luke Rodgers, last year's young superstar, having his feet kept firmly on the ground by being given the twelfth-man role of carrying the drinks crate across the pitch at half-time. He looked cheerful enough.

Two reporters were sitting behind me during the second half. I don't know what papers they represented, but they seemed unfamiliar with the Shrewsbury team. "Who's the number 15, who just came on?" one inquired of the other. Most of the inhabitants of Rochdale would know it was Luke Rodgers, but apparently not this man.

"Do you realise that the number 7 hasn't even got his name on the team listed in the programme?" I offered.

"Who?"

"Ryan Lowe."

"Yes, I've got him and the number 11."

He was referring to Steve Jagielka who had by now been substituted. "But can you spell his name?" I challenged.

"We just put in plenty of Cs and Ks," he replied.

Would that classify as racist? I wondered.

I had spotted Chris Smith as I entered the ground. You don't get many points for that, as he goes to every Salop game. He's pretty well known in the world of STFC, having organised coaches for away travel over many years, and even shares the honour with Arthur Rowley of being a Life Member of the Club. He's the sort of genuine fanatic whose time, enthusiasm and commitment mean so much to football clubs. They're part of an invaluable unpaid infrastructure. He also owns what is probably the most impressive collection of Salop matchday programmes on this planet.

Lennie's Great Escape

Pre-season

"And we all know that in football if you stand still you go backwards." – Peter Reid

Because I don't live in Shrewsbury much of the New Meadow debate passes me by. I do, however, look on the internet and tune in to Radio Shropshire. Today I heard Town Director Keith Sayfritz say they planned to have conference facilities at the New Meadow. Let's hope he didn't mean Conference facilities.

One of the main problems for anyone writing about football is the sheer volume of words that are continuously produced on the subject. Every day, in season and out, they fill the tabloids and glossy magazines. They flood the airwaves as inevitably as the Severn does Shrewsbury, and leave behind comparable filth, destruction and misery. These words bounce off satellites. They rumble around pubs. There are enough ghosted biographies of players and managers every year to rival the turnout of spirits on Halloween. This means that a cliché is always waiting to hijack the next phrase. How many ways are there of expressing elation (the over-the-moon emotion) or despair (the sick-as-a-parrot or "gutted" end of the spectrum)? Each goal may be unique, but the number of adjectives, adverbs and verbs is finite, even in our wonderful multi-synonymed English language.

Reminders of Shrewsbury Town crop up from time to time in my everyday life in Birmingham. I was intrigued a few years back to see a youth living just down the road from me actually wearing one of the "scrambled egg" shirts from 1992-3. (As intrigued as when I realised that one of the characters in *This is Spinal Tap* was wearing a shirt from the 1980-1982 era.) This would be a strange fashion statement at the best of times, but would take a lot of bottle on an estate in Birmingham. On another occasion I visited a local primary school only to be introduced to a young teacher sipping from a Shrewsbury Town mug. – Good taste indeed.

If these coincidences amazed me, they were nothing compared to what happened when I was a young teacher, keen, energetic and having nothing better to do with most of my evenings and Saturday mornings than to manage a school football team. As I was running up and down the touchline exhorting my charges to greater efforts, I became aware of a strange phenomenon. The teacher from the other school was coaching his team by making reference to names and tactics of a League team, and that team was Shrewsbury Town. "Come on, Roberts! Get down that line and centre for Wood!"

Last year's floods brought a whole new meaning to: "Shrewsbury were forced to use all their subs."

Other pre-season games in July before the Bridgnorth trip were as follows:
14th July 2001 friendly versus Burscough (away); Lost 1-0.
17th July 2001 friendly versus Connah's Quay (away); Won 1-0 (Freestone).

After the Bridgnorth game Salop embarked on a mini-tour of South Wales, the results being:
21st July 2001 friendly versus Merthyr Tydfil (away); Won 3-1 (Lowe, Jemson, Atkins).
25th July 2001 friendly versus Newport County (away); Won 3-0 (Walker 2, Jagielka).

The other pre-season games were closer to home:
28th August 2001 friendly versus Wolverhampton Wanderers (home);

Lost 2-0.
1st August 2001 Shropshire Senior Cup versus Telford United (away); Won 3-1 (Jagielka 2, Wilding).

I don't get to many pre-season games – in fact only a handful over the years. I remember a game at Hereford when I was a student earning coppers picking blackcurrants nearby. Salop scored five that day, mainly through a rampant Alf Wood. The legendary John Charles was still the Hereford manager, but his playing days were over. I also recall a game against Stoke when 5,000 turned up at the Gay Meadow expecting to see Gordon Banks but got only John Farmer. This must have been just after the 1970 World Cup, which I still think England were good enough to have won. The Salopian admirers of Banks may not have got to see their hero in action but at least we won, which is more than the experience enjoyed by the good people who turned up to watch Manchester United's reserves demolish the Town last year. It is also more than I got from watching a metamorphosing Jake King Salop side play Tranmere a couple of years ago. Pre-season friendlies are awkward affairs. Not only do the times and locations tend to be inconvenient, but the games are experimental in terms of players and strategy and furthermore they are almost as non-competitive as benefit games. At least Shropshire Senior Cup games against Telford United seem to have some purpose and bite.

Home Thoughts from Abroad

"And the news from Guadalajara where the temperature is 96 degrees, is that Falcao is warming up." – Brian Moore

I missed the only pre-season friendly played at home this year. The day Salop played Wolves I was travelling to Austria, but such is the power that football exerts on the mind that as I was sitting to dinner several hundreds of miles from Shropshire, with the Alps outside clothed in their customary awesome beauty and crickets fiddling away merrily, I was wondering what the score had been in what would have been a fairly meaningless football game in the English Midlands.

While I was on holiday I watched a little football on TV. If nothing else, this served to remind me of how slow we are in this country to adapt to changes in the game as far as language is concerned. The German commentator was referring to the ball hitting the aluminium. Any British commentator would still talk of it hitting "the woodwork". I don't know what they call assistant referees in German, but the politically incorrect Shrewsbury crowd invariably target their abuse at the "linesman". To my knowledge there may have been female assistant referees at Telford, but not yet at Shrewsbury.

What is often overlooked about Third Division football is the level of skill. To anyone taking a superficial look, or in the minds of those who have never bothered to take a look, it can seem mostly a matter of kick and clog, one set of ineptitude and mediocrity cancelling out another, a tale full of sound and fury; but I have watched with wonder at the degree of control that someone like Ryan Lowe exercises over the ball (he can trap it and have it where he wants it with consummate and deceptive ease) or the seemingly instinctive defence-splitting passes that Nigel Jemson produces every now and then. The only football skill the majority of ordinary people could perform better than Nigel is to fall over convincingly in the penalty area.

There is a lot of superstition in football and that includes the idea of bogey teams. As far as I'm concerned Shrewsbury's bogey team is Rotherham United. Their record in run-of-the-mill games might not suggest this. Indeed in League games we outshine them: in twenty-one seasons of competing in the same Division we have won at home on eleven occasions and away eight times; they have only won at home eight times and away five times. Moreover, we knocked them out of the FA Cup in 1982-3. However, in the games that matter it's a different story. What have been arguably Salop's two biggest footballing moments have been ruined by Rotherham. In recent times, on the only occasion Salop have ever reached Wembley, it was Rotherham who beat us there – with, of course, the added irony that the Rotherham goals were both scored by a certain Nigel Jemson. By now it is a distant memory (or perhaps news to younger fans) that

Salop almost made it to the final of the first ever League Cup in 1960-1 (admittedly before all the "big guns" were taking part) to play Aston Villa. But in the semi-final over two legs, after extra time, we lost to Rotherham United 4-3. Ironically, in these days of away goals counting double we would have gone through on the strength of the two goals we scored in Rotherham, but then it was not to be. They also defeated us when we met at the Meadow in the same competition in 1965-6 – by a mere 2-5 that time.

I welcome these days of improved communication. *The Shropshire Star* is fine as far as general news and reports of games are concerned, but because of the nature of newspapers it can not tell distant fans if a game is called off late in the day, and the level of interaction is limited to whatever letters it chooses to publish (and edit). By "improved communication" I am referring mainly to the Internet, which provides instant, up-to-date, relevant news in an attractive user-friendly format. It also allows for involvement and feedback from supporters. The official Town site is good, but the Blue-and-amber site is superb. In contrast the "Town Talk" 0891 telephone information of a couple of years back was not only amateurish and rarely up-to-the-minute, but was also a rip-off, with someone (— the Clubs or a telephone company?) making a big profit out of football fans. These taped broadcasts would consist of a lot of unnecessary and repetitive pre-amble, mostly self-advertising, whilst any useful information was deliberately and tantalisingly kept back until the poor fan had run up an exorbitant telephone bill. This was no improvement on the days when you could try ringing the Club directly to ascertain whether a game was still on. At least then you might get the current state of affairs, although I have turned up on at least two occasions in the past to find that the match had been cancelled (in the case of a benefit game) or postponed. When I wrote to the Club secretary, Malcolm Starkey, to complain about the appalling communication of information and how it affected those not living locally he offered little sympathy.

As I said above, whilst on holiday I watched a number of games on

TV, including Newcastle United versus 1860 München. Lua-lua, Newcastle's forward (born in Kinshasa but a Congo international), scored a nice little goal when he pounced on a defender's mistake just outside the box, went wide as the goalkeeper charged out, and slid the ball in from the acutest of angles. What particularly struck me about this game was the amount of awful thuggery that went completely unpunished by the referee. TV has a habit of dwelling on such incidents, repeating them from every angle, revelling in the teeth-jarring barbarity.

It is also my experience that television is a belittling medium, reducing moments of skill to commonplace failure. The camera loves a David Beckham free kick but treats near misses as scarce worth comment. I rarely see a game live and then also in a televised version, but I remember a Walsall versus Shrewsbury game in which Jimmy Lindsay (Salop 1977-81; a player whose skills rarely stirred even the most partisan supporter) took a free kick that skimmed the wood-work (it possibly was wood-work in those days) and brought an animated reaction from the crowd. I later saw TV highlights that made Lindsay's kick look technically inept and inaccurate in the execution.

A football club is not the chairman, directors, manager, coaches or players. Any of these, for good or ill, might (and only might) have an influence on the way a club develops – whether it gets promoted or relegated, whether it plays with a particular ethos or style, whether it communicates well with and involves its fans, whether it is financially stable or bankrupt. They are all, however, temporary, merely caretakers of their roles, trustees and executors of the club. At Shrewsbury Town, since joining the League, the record for a chairman is Tim Yates at twenty years; whilst there have been some eighteen managers (if we include Ken Brown who can be credited with a mere week at the helm), the longest serving being Arthur Rowley at ten years, and it is not a club renowned for its boardroom strife or readiness to sack a manager at the first sign of a few poor results. There have been some long-serving players, though none probably surpass Colin Griffin, who put in almost five hundred first team appearances in a variety of competitions between 1976 and 1988, or

Mickey Brown, who started as an apprentice in 1986 and (with a couple of breaks for good behaviour) saw the Town through thick and thin before finally being released in 2001. If you measure these terms with what a fan puts in they are brief indeed. True fans have an allegiance for life. Even those whose attendance at games varies according to the team's success, or whose attendance is limited by geography, are probably committed to the club in spirit for far longer than a player's career. My own brother, for example, now lives outside Shropshire and has long ago lost the habit of attending football matches of any grade; however, he still knows how Salop are faring and usually has more of a viewpoint than me on what is going on. It is the fans that are the club's soul, that tend and nurture the flame of the club's spirit; but this is a collective matter and Saturday will keep coming after the individual fan has taken up a season ticket in Heaven.

Evidence of my brother's continued interest is contained in the following letter I received in May 2000...

"Having, like any right-thinking person, given up any hope of salvation, I had determined not even to look at the results of Saturday's games in order to avoid unnecessary gloom, but when clearing away the papers on Sunday evening I happened to glimpse: [clip from top of *The Sunday Times* Sport section with picture of a cavorting celebrating huddle of Town players (Brown, Wilding, Jagielka, Tretton) and the heading "Escape to victory: Shrewsbury avoid the drop"] – that's the trouble these days, the sport doesn't confine itself to the back page and you can find it lurking all over the place.

"The only positive thought that I'd had was that they were playing Exeter. It's always been Exeter. They had to beat them to leapfrog over Swansea and Watford, and wasn't it Exeter when Arthur took them out of Div 4? At least, they had to beat them in the last-but-one game, then play Watford again after the floodlight failure.

"I don't suppose you went? If 1500 really did, that must be the whole crowd of regulars. It's amazing how relegation brings them out – more than the prospect of going up ever did.

"It's just a pity about Chester. I think Carlisle deserved it more."

That Frank knows all about the history of vital encounters between Salop and Exeter proves my point. These are just not the sort of facts that are at the finger-tips of the casual observer. I would just add that there is something in what he says about the phenomenon of impending relegation bringing out the crowds for the final game. I have memories of being in a crowd of 30,000 to watch Aston Villa relegated to the Third Division.

Everton is another club of particular interest in the history of Shrewsbury Town. Salop knocked Everton out of the first ever League Cup (with two goals from Peter Dolby). Everton had to wait until the Eighties to avenge that defeat, but did so with relish. They beat us 4-1 at the Meadow in the 1985-6 League Cup. We have also played them twice in the FA Cup in consecutive years, when they have triumphed. Both of these were at Goodison and the first one (1982-3) was on a Sunday which meant that Bernard McNally, arguably the lynchpin of the Salop team at that time, wouldn't play because of his religious convictions. Mind you, it didn't help much when he did play the following year, as we lost 3-0 that time. These were occasions when Gary Stevens lined up against Gary Stevens. I went to both games with Frank who at the time was teaching in Liverpool. For the first game I think he had commissioned a pupil to get us tickets, so we were sitting in the middle of Everton fans. I can remember he needed to restrain me when Steve Cross scored for Salop with what the exaggeration of time stretches to a forty yarder.

What was the first football game I saw? I was five and had to go into hospital for an operation. As luck would have it, in those days the Royal Salop Infirmary was in the building on the top of the bank overlooking the Gay Meadow from the town side (it is now occupied by the Parade Shopping Centre). So in October 1953, from the vantage point of a balcony high above the Severn – a bit like the view that these people have from windows, roofs and balconies overlooking Test Match grounds – I watched Shrewsbury Town beat

Southend United 2-1, with goals from Edwin Beynon and Frederick Fisher. I cannot pretend to remember the details of the game, but I probably had a reasonable view of most of the pitch, given the height and the fact that the poplar trees lining the Severn at the back of the Riverside Stand would not have been above the roof of the stand then. Whatever else, it must surely have been a defining moment.

Let's clear up the matter of the sheep (even though as a Shrewsbury Town supporter sheep are one topic that I hesitate to bring up).... A couple of years back there was an indignant mention in either a matchday programme or one of the fanzines (and I cannot remember which now) of some allegedly calumnious statement about sheep in a field outside the ground. If whoever was protesting against this had looked just outside the ground they would have seen that sheep were indeed grazing on the grass below the former Royal Salop Infirmary.

What was the first football I saw on TV? That would have been the 1958 World Cup Final between Sweden and Brazil, which Brazil won 5-2. We did not have a television in those days so I saw this on a neighbour's set. It was a brilliant game won by a brilliant team, and just the sort to confirm a football mad boy into following Pele's beautiful game and to know that if other sides could not always provide it in its purest form then Pele's nation's side could usually be relied upon (although, it must be said, Brazil have had their share of hard men who have not so beautifully stood behind and provided protection for those who have used the ball as poets use words).

How fanatical a fan am I? At the time of writing I do not possess, let alone wear, a replica kit. I have no blue and amber fluffy dice or miniature boots dangling annoyingly and dangerously from the mirror in my car. My keys are not on a STFC key-ring. I have no stickers in my car or the front windows of my house. I have no "loggerheads" nose-stud. I have never decorated my bedroom with pictures of footballers nor painted the front of the house blue and amber. I have never taken a banner, hooter or rattle to a match. The only scarf I wear is a reminder of student days rather than a token of tribal football allegiance. I do have two Shrewsbury Town mugs and a Blue and Amber account with the West Bromwich Building Society. I have never possessed a season ticket. I do not travel to all away games – in fact, hardly any. I do not even manage to go to all home games, particularly on weekday evenings or during holiday periods. Does all this make me any less of a fan? I like to believe that for me football is an interest not an obsession. There is a distinction between monomania and commitment. Perhaps a true indicator of allegiance is that I would have been devastated had the Club dropped out of the League at the end of that awful 1999-2000 season. I felt that I ought to go to the final game at Exeter, but ultimately couldn't even bear to keep watching Teletext to the bitter end.

From time to time they have "meet the players" functions or opportunities to be using the players' lounge. That sort of thing doesn't really attract me. I think you need a distance between players and fans. Players don't need to feel they're public property all the time or virtually stalker-victims. Why should we concern ourselves with the trivia of their lives – their habits, hobbies, experiences, preferences and opinions. As a fan, I want to watch footballers doing what they're good at (and what they're paid for) – hopefully, playing football. If I want to discuss the works of Dickens or whether Britain should adopt the Euro, I would look to other interlocutors. Being a gifted football player does not mean that he will have the answer to everything or even know how to run his own life. – Who in their right mind would take advice from Vic Kasule, late of this parish (yet what a thrilling footballer to watch)? Should we hero-worship drunks, flashers, kerb-crawlers or those who make the front-page of the tabloids for the wrong reasons (are there any right reasons?)? Can we divorce the footballing personality from the non-footballing public persona and/or private truth? Get too close to an idol and see the feet of clay. According to a teacher at the Wakeman School there is an embarrassment factor involved in working at the school; namely that of hearing through the classroom windows the somewhat colourful language of the footballers as they train. Maybe that is close enough.

The nearest I have gone in the direction of making contact with players before undertaking this book was when as a student I combined my interest in textual study (by spending a couple of days looking at rare versions of F.Scott Fitzgerald texts in the British Library) with my interest in football by hiking down to Brighton to watch Brighton and Hove Albion versus Salop. It was at the old Goldstone ground and in the days before segregated crowds and I can remember being near a middle-aged female Brighton fan who spent the entire game informing Trevor Meredith (of all people) what a dirty player he was. Town weren't brilliant and lost 3-0. After the game, I collected autographs as the players came out to the team coach (some via the chip-shop – oh, the glamour of Third Division football). There are signatures from John Phillips, Tony Gregory, George Boardman, Peter Dolby, Denis Hawkins, Pat Douglas (a collector's item?) and Jimmy McLaughlin, who even added the number 11 to make it clear who he was. The one omission that I regretted at the time was that of Alf Wood, who was obviously not into signing autographs. Ironically Alf was the only ex-Salop player I had met away from football grounds (if you discount the odd sighting of George Boardman in Shrewsbury and Carl Griffiths in Oswestry; and not forgetting listening to a few "Well, Brian" statements liberally laced with f-words from George Andrews when he caught the train to Dudley as we were going back to Wellington [My brother comments: "I didn't think George was that bad and I liked the way he got out his Pools coupon."]. In recent years in connection with his business Alf has visited the school where I teach in Birmingham. I have exchanged a few pleasantries with him, but I still haven't got his autograph.

The perks (not Steve) of following Salop may be far between and few, but I did benefit from one that not many fans will have experienced outside those supporting teams that make a habit of getting into FA Cup Finals. In 1970 my persistence in going to virtually all the Home games at the Gay Meadow was rewarded by a ticket for one of the most memorable FA Cup Finals of all time. I don't think this still happens, but the basic idea was that by sending in tokens from the matchday programmes one was entered in a draw. For once in my life I was lucky and witnessed Chelsea pulling off an unlikely draw against the all-conquering team of the moment, Leeds United (the history books tell us that they then went on to the even more unlikely feat of winning the replay). That Leeds team was magnificent, a marvellous mixture of barely controlled aggression and wonderful skill (typified perhaps by Billy Bremner); they had an Achilles' heel, however, in the form of their goalkeeper, Gary Oops Sprake.

Leeds United also featured in one of the most exciting live games I have ever attended (excepting of course any game at the Gay Meadow). They were playing Manchester United at Villa Park in an FA Cup Semi-final; and, although I say it was one of the most exciting games I have seen, strangely there were no goals. Part of the excitement may have been down to the adrenalin rush caused by being in a crowd that would respond to any moment of thrilling action by surging forward. This was in the days before the Holte End was all-seats, so one was carried yards in a flow of helpless movement the like of which I have not experienced elsewhere, nor would wish to do so. It was somewhat like being at a pop concert where the crowd pushes towards the stage, but with greater numbers. It was I suppose a preview of the several unfortunate incidents that led ultimately to the great revision of safety measures in football stadia.

Incidentally, if you consider Germans to be somewhat cold, humourless and unemotional, maybe their language is partly responsible [I am put in mind of this, surrounded as I am currently by German-speakers]. The language often does not allow them to have direct feelings. It is as though Germans do not feel emotion, they have it played upon them. Emotions are expressed through grammatically passive not active forms. Thus they can't say "I'm sorry", they have to say "Es tut mir leid" (it makes me sorry); similarly not "I am pleased" but "Es gefällt mir" (it pleases me); and "Es geht mir gut" (it goes well to/for me) not "I am well".

Let's clear up this "Salop" thing. For the uninitiated, it is not the French insult (with the alternative spelling of "salaud"); it comes from the Mediaeval Latin "Salopia" (as in the alternative title of this book, sort of) and can refer to both Shropshire and Shrewsbury. In this book it is used exclusively to refer to Shrewsbury Town Football Club.

Football enthusiasts delight in devising hypothetical teams: an imaginary Arsenal team of Welshmen, an Arsenal team of Frenchmen, the best eleven left-footed Arsenal players, a team of Arsenal players born under the sign of Virgo, a team of non-smoking Arsenal players, a team of Arsenal players who have conquered Mount Everest, and so on. Mike Jones, in his magnificent tome *Breathe on 'em Salop*, came up with Salop teams for each decade from the 1950's onwards, teams of loan players, black players, players who made only one appearance, and players who played for Town and whose brothers also made League appearances – fascinating if a trifle cerebral.

In this tradition, how about the following for a team of ex-Salop players who have also been managers of League teams? –

Mike Walker (Norwich etc)
Jake King (Salop)
Asa Hartford (Salop)
David Moyes (Preston/Everton)
Nigel Pearson (Carlisle)
Alan Durban (Salop)
Graham Turner (Salop etc)
David Pleat (Luton etc)
Ian Atkins (Carlisle etc)
Arthur Rowley (Salop etc)
Chic Bates (Salop etc)

Or what about the following for a squad of Alans who have played for Salop? –
Boswell (1963-8), Humphreys (1956-60), Wakeman (1953-4), Jones (1968), Durban (1973-8), Irvine (1988-9), Brown (1982-4), Turner (1966-7), Tarbuck (1973-6), Walsh (1992), Cockrane (1974), Finley (1988-90), Groves (1971-2).

I offer this as a squad rather than a team because with three goal-keepers but no other real defenders it is a little unbalanced for a team and they would need to sort themselves out. I have also picked a squad of my all-time favourite Salop players, which I will introduce one at a time as the book progresses, occasionally accompanied by some response from the player. The selection of such a team is comparable to choosing the poems for an anthology; the anthologist likes them, but other people quibble about why some have been included whilst others that they see as more meritorious have been omitted. – “Good grief! He’s gone for the Ancient Mariner and spurned the Faerie Queene.” so to speak. It’s the sort of debate that will enliven pub conversation for many years to come.

The Squad August 2001

“Paneira with his unmistakeble style...but no, it’s not him.” – Portuguese Commentator

Goalkeepers

Ian Dunbavin

Born Huyton. A young keeper who learned his trade in the Liverpool youth set-up, playing behind Michael Owen, Jamie Carragher and Steven Gerrard. Part of the Liverpool team that won the FA Youth Cup, but more importantly kept goal for Salop in the historic victory at Exeter.

Mark Cartwright

Signed at the start of this season as a replacement for the long-serving Paul Edwards. Born in Chester. Has spent time previously with York City, Stockport County, Wrexham and Brighton (— Does a list get any more impressive than that?). Seized the goalkeeper’s jersey following a pre-season injury to Ian Dunbavin.

Defenders

Iain Jenkins

Northern Ireland international full-back, but currently struggling to hang onto a place in the Salop starting line. Signed from Dundee United a year ago. (Next stop: Dr Marten's?)

Greg Rioch

Born in Sutton Coldfield. Will probably always suffer from being referred to as the son of Bruce Rioch. Is himself a solid if unspectacular left back who likes to get forward and cross the ball into the box. An apprentice at Millwall where his father was manager, he has since been at Luton, Barnet, Peterborough, Hull and Macclesfield (captaining the last two). With Salop from March 2001.

Matthew Redmile

Words such as "solid" and "uncompromising" cling to this young man. A commanding figure at the heart of the defence, but very effective in the opposition's penalty area. Played over 150 games for home-town club Notts County, from whom he was signed in January 2001 after a loan period.

Mick Heathcote

Born in the North East. He signed for Sunderland from Spennymoor. After loan spells at Halifax and York he signed for Salop (£55,000). He is now starting his second spell at the Gay Meadow having been here previously for the 1990-1 season. In the interim he has been with Cambridge (who paid £150,000) and Plymouth. He was a very popular and successful centre-half the first time he was here. It is to be hoped that his maturity will outweigh the advancing years.

Andrew Tretton

Born in Derby. Signed from Derby County in December 1997. Currently out of favour and likely to be behind Redmile and Heathcote in the central-defender pecking order. However, while Jake King was in charge, he was the captain, a post he retained as far as the club's relegation escape at Exeter.

Peter Wilding
One of those rare creatures, a Salop player born in Shrewsbury. He was, however, a late entrant to professional football and is making the most of the opportunity now. He played non-league football for Bridgnorth, Newtown and Telford before signing for Salop in 1997 at the age of 27. He is a utility player in the true sense, making a committed effort wherever he is played.

Leon Drysdale
Born Walsall. Though a Schoolboy with Wolves, he is a graduate from the Salop Youth team, which he captained. A right back, he made his League debut at home to Rotherham in April 1999.

Kevin Seabury
Another Shrewsbury-born player. Joined the club straight from school and has played almost 300 times, mainly as right back. Popular with the fans for his wholehearted commitment to the club, but not in favour with the management.

Darren Moss
Born in Wrexham, but he's all right now. A Welsh Youth International, he plays at right back or in midfield. Signed for Salop from Chester at the start of the season.

Jamie Tolley

Born in Ludlow. A terrific prospect who became Salop's youngest ever first team player when he came on as substitute against Oxford United on 20th November 1999 (at the age of 16 years 193 days). Has represented Wales at Under-21 level.

Karl Murray

London-born but moved to Cannock as a teenager, Karl is another product of the Town's youth policy. Made his senior debut on 10th August 1999 at the age of 17 against Sheffield United.

Mark Atkins

Born Doncaster. A seasoned pro, who could reach 600 appearances if he plays in most of the games this season. He is one of few (if not the only) player signed by Salop to have been transferred for a million. He represented England Schoolboys and made his League debut for Scunthorpe United at 16 years 8 months. Made over 300 appearances for Blackburn (including winning the Premier League title alongside Shearer and Batty in 1994-5). Moved to Wolves (for the million), then York City (on a free transfer), out of the League with Doncaster Rovers and back in with Hull City. Signed for Salop at the start of the season.

Josh Walker

19 year old Brummie, recently signed from Manchester United. Gave up on challenging for a place in the United midfield and might struggle to establish himself here.

Midfielders/Forwards

Sam Aiston

A winger, born in Newcastle. He was a Newcastle United trainee and an England Schools player. Signed for Salop from Sunderland in July 2000 for £50,000 after initially coming on loan. Also had loan spells at Chester and Stoke. Exciting when in full flow and taking men on, but still needs to make the end product count.

Steve Jagielka

Born in Manchester, he was a schoolboy with Manchester City and became a trainee at Stoke. Signed from Stoke in July 1997. Speedy and hard-working.

Forwards

Luke Rodgers

Yet another to come through Town's Youth system, this young Brummie is our bright hope – first to score lots of goals to secure promotion, and second to attract so much attention from Premier clubs that he will bring in millions to the Town's needy coffers. Though diminutive he is aggressive and a natural goalscorer. He is a natural foil for Nigel Jemson. Most memorable moment to date is his hat-trick (and sending-off for the consequent shirt-removing celebration) in last season's 7 – 1 away trouncing of Rochdale. Scored 7 goals in 13 starts last season. Should do even better this year.

Nigel Jemson

Another seasoned and much travelled pro (more clubs than….). He represented England at Under-21 level. He scored the winning goal for Nottingham Forest in the 1990 Littlewoods Cup Final and we won't mention Rotherham versus Shrewsbury at Wembley (though, who knows, perhaps someday he will atone for that by doing a Peter Dolby against Everton and thereby achieving legendary status himself). His list of clubs is roughly as follows: Preston, Nottingham Forest, Bolton, Sheffield Wednesday (for £800,000), Grimsby, Notts County, Oxford, Watford, Coventry, Rotherham, Bury, Ayr, Oxford (again). He joined Salop at the start of last season and as well as being the leading scorer (with 15) he is also the captain.

Ryan Lowe
Born Liverpool. Signed from Burscough (for whom he had been a prolific scorer) at the start of last season. A live-wire on the pitch.

Chris Freestone
Born in Nottingham. Moved from non-league Arnold Town to Middlesbrough, but didn't really establish himself. Also with Northampton and Hartlepool (and on loan to Cheltenham). Signed on a free transfer from Hartlepool at the start of last season. Does well in pre-season but has yet to hit a rich vein of scoring.

Chris Murphy
Another young striker (the next Luke Rodgers?). Made his debut at the age of 18 on the final day of last season at home to Brighton.

15th August, 2001
"then ye contented your souls / With the flannelled fools at the wicket or the muddied oafs at the goals." — Rudyard Kipling

Today I received a letter from Roland Wycherley, the Town Chairman. – Oh, all right, it was only a photocopied circular, nothing personal. It offered me, as a supporter, a free replica team shirt if I took up an offer to subscribe to ITV Digital. That's all well and good, but much as I like football and television I don't want to be a slave to either or both. If I am one of the football enthusiasts they were counting on when they signed their multi-million deal, they are likely to come unstuck. The thought of watching football on television every night of the week is horrifying. I would like to feel that life had more to offer. The idea of subscribing to digital or satellite or cable television is also less than attractive. We should be aiming for quality programmes on the television channels we have, not submitting to a proliferation of channels just so that someone can make money. I've been in countries where they have this so-called choice and all it serves is to make channel-hopping a candidate as an Olympic event.

Saturday 18th August, 2001
"I never comment on referees and I'm not going to break the habit of a lifetime for that prat." – Ron Atkinson

Hartlepool United (home); Football League Division Three

Previous record in league games					
Home			Away		
Win	Draw	Lose	Win	Draw	Lose
3	3	3	2	3	4

1-3 (HT 1-0); Rodgers (40)
Attendance: 2,783
Standpoint: For most of the game, on the Riverside, leaning against a barrier just in front of the band; for the last few minutes, on the Wakeman End.

First home game of the season and high expectations, partly because most seasons start like that until reality sets in (roughly thirty minutes into the first game) and partly because of last week's startling result at Plymouth. Despite playing much of the game with only ten men (Karl Murray sent off) the Town managed to win 1-0, courtesy of a Nigel Jemson tap in when the ball was knocked back into the box after a corner. Those few, largely indisputable facts, I gleaned from Teletext and the *Sunday Mercury*; I also caught the goal on television. I don't usually bother to read detailed match reports, on the grounds that when I have read ones of games that I have seen they often come over as biased and selective, extolling the praises of players who were rarely involved and even getting the atmosphere and the balance of play completely wrong. A hundred thousand spectators at the same match will see a hundred thousand different games. So if I'm at a game I don't need to read about it. If I wasn't there, then the result and scorers are all that matter, unless there was something unusual – pitch invaded by goats, cross-bar snapped in two, mass-brawl by players, fire in the buffet, those sorts of thing – or it is for some reason a special match (for example, Auto Windshield Cup Final at Wembley 1996; last game of the season nail-biter, Exeter 2000; Town score SEVEN at Rochdale 2001). Having said this, because of what I am doing this year, I may possibly be looking at newspaper accounts more often.

I love this place. At the moment the Gay Meadow itself may be somewhat down-at-heel, but can there be anywhere a more beautiful setting? The stadium (which, as anyone in Shrewsbury knows, takes its name from the field it is built on, the Gaye Meadow – so named when it belonged to the Abbey in the Middle Ages) lies beside the serene Severn (all right, so it floods occasionally), where the English Bridge crosses over. It stands just outside the river loop around the finest of mediæval towns. From one of my favoured standpoints I can look up and see the Abbey. As I walk along the terraces on the Wakeman End I can see the quaint Laura's Tower, which Thomas Telford added to the Castle a couple of hundred years ago for Sir William Pulteney, after whose wife it is named. Trains go past, slowing (to watch the game or to pull up to the platform?) – occasionally a steam engine. In autumn the leaves from the colonnade of poplars lining the river at the back of the stadium blow over the Riverside Stand and strew the pitch. Over the years I have stood or sat in every part of this ground – maybe not the directors' box, the press-box, the dug-outs, or even the match sponsor's enclosure, but everywhere else. In the days before crowds were segregated I was often at the Station End, and it is ironic that my earliest memories of the "Salop Choir" are that it was not in the middle of the Riverside as now but at the Station End where the opposition have been penned for these many years. The worst period as a spectator was when they put up fences. Thank god, sense prevailed and they finally got rid of them (except on the Station End), having first as an intermediate stage trimmed the tops to allow better views.

On the subject of Karl Murray, I wonder whether this could be his season. He came into the team a couple of years ago and looked very promising. Last year he struggled to get a look-in (or was being brought on more cautiously). If he has started off in favour, maybe he will get settled (unless suspension spoils that for him).

So here am I with my first raw throat of the season from shouting, mostly for the wrong reasons – and in the middle of a holiday, with not even the frustration of work to exorcise....

Before the game, a great deal of eager anticipation.... first home game of the season; the team had won their opening game last Saturday; a strong looking team. So, maybe the sun wasn't shining and it looked like being a damp afternoon, but this is an English summer, albeit the fag-end.

The afternoon had started so well. It was a lovely touch that the team mascot for the day should be Charlie Jemson, Nigel's son. The three-piece band (drum, trombone and, I think, trumpet) were on the Riverside for the first time playing such favourites as the Great Escape, which earned its significance in 2000, and Bladon Races, which of course has its own Shrewsbury lyrics ("Ooh my lads / You should have seen their faces, / Coming down the Wyle Cop / To see the Shrewsbury aces"). Though much of the first half was perhaps a little lacklustre, the only team creating anything was the Town. The back looked solid, particularly centrally; the midfield was industrious and in control; and the forwards were linking well. It livened up towards the end of the half, with a stunning goal from Luke Rodgers.

At 2 o'clock the world looked a delightful, if damp, place. Reading the match-day programme, I noted that Chris Smith was sponsoring the matchball in memory of his grandfather, Sam Powell, who had been the Club's trainer, physio, president of the supporters' club and a director. So Chris Smith's connection with the Club goes back a long time.

Anyway.... as I was saying, by the time the second half was ready to get under way the world looked a delightful, if damp, place. I was musing on the success of Kevin Ratcliffe's strategy of playing a spine of very experienced players (Heathcote, Atkins, Jemson) with young legs around them to do the nipping, zipping, harrying and carrying. Then the wheels fell off....

The old "game of two halves" might be a cliché, but that's what this was. Within minutes of the re-start the referee had sent off Redmile, sent off Atkins, awarded Hartlepool a penalty, started taking throw-ins and hacking down what was left of the Shrewsbury midfield. – All right, I'm lying about the last couple of items on the list, but only so far as literal truth is concerned. Figuratively speaking he may just as well have been doing those things for he had single-handedly destroyed the game as a competitive spectacle and as entertainment. The crowd chanted "Three-one to the referee", and they were right. Matt Redmile was sent off for a second bookable offence, the first of which was a robust tackle that would often go unpunished and in which it could be argued he actually played the ball. I don't know why Mark Atkins was sent off. And the penalty was for the sort of manœuvre that is often classified as a dive. At one man down, with the dependable and versatile Peter Wilding (he's played pretty much everywhere, including in goals) – with Wilding slotting back into central defence, Town could like last week have survived, but two men down is a different matter, and although they battled well it was only a case of how long they could hold out. The rain had persisted and perhaps there was significance in the fact that the yellow paint freshly applied to mark where one should not stand on the terraces was beginning to run.

I appreciate that referees have the toughest of jobs and I do not in the least envy them. However, this was a game between two teams of professionals watched by almost three thousand people, including me, who had paid to be entertained. Through his incompetence (and maybe arrogance also comes into it) that man had robbed Salop of three points that could prove crucial by the end of the season and had robbed me of £10. If I wanted to see farce I'd go to see Brian Rix (or whoever currently gets paid for running around in public without their trousers). If I wanted to watch injustice in action I'd get a season ticket for the Old Bailey. The chant of "Cheat! Cheat!" at the final whistle referred as much as anything to what the crowd felt had been done to them.

This is not the first time I have seen a game of this nature. The one versus Cardiff at the Meadow in March 2001 was another that springs to mind, when the appalling lack of action by the referee in the face of some brutal and cynical play from Cardiff caused Nigel Jemson to flip his lid and get himself sent off just before half-time and Steve Jagielka was sent off in the second half. If I remember correctly, Kevin Ratcliffe was probably "sent off" too.

Referees must be up to the job or they should not be doing it. It is the worst thing about Third Division football – a decent referee is like snow in August. Does it have to be the training ground for would-be Premiership referees? It is certainly significant that the referees for these two first games were both new to the league. Was the problem their inexperience, or their feeling that they needed to prove themselves, or that they have not been adequately trained in how to exercise good sense in the interpretation of the rules of the game and in applying appropriate measures – though having said that, in the following week David Ellery had a similar effect on a game between Everton and Spurs and there were a few other interesting dismissals in the Premier League. What they need are a few referees like my mate Chas who would not stand for any funny business on the indiscipline front but does have a sense of humour.

If I (and a couple of thousand other spectators) feel so angry about what happened this afternoon, how must Kevin Ratcliffe feel? It is after all his livelihood, his life. He has assembled a squad, trained them, gathered information, thought out tactics, seen things taking shape, only for a *deus ex machina* to intervene. Football managers live or die by the results of their team. It is no wonder that at one point Mr Ratcliffe and the referee were eyeball to eyeball on the touchline. By then the referee had obviously lost it (if he ever knew what it was) and Kevin Ratcliffe must have said a few words from the heart. It's the most fundamental taboo of football: if thou art a manager thou shalt not criticise the referee.

Neither are Salop a dirty team. Matthew Redmile is hard, but that's what a centre-half is. Yet what sort of reputation will they have? — Three sent off in the first two games. I abhor violence, but there is a distinction between malicious violence and combative, competitive, aggression. Referees must not just be taught the rules of the game, they also need training in man management and how to ensure that they do not ruin a game by being over-intrusive or unnecessarily heavy handed. A quiet word at the right moment will often prove more effective control of a game than coloured cards flourished willy-nilly.

The other point about games like this is the reporting of them. Those who were there know the truth. The national newspapers will report with bland facts. Apart from dishonourable mention in fanzines and on fan-run websites, the only written criticism of this referee will probably be Kevin Ratcliffe's report and the Football League (or is it the FA that deals with these matters?) will just file that under "No action to be taken" or "Ratcliffe's rantings" or put it down to "bad loser". I will be interested in what the *Shropshire Star* has to say, whether it will reflect the perceptions of the fans and club.

These are not just the ravings of a biased mind [although Frank opines that they sound just that]. I admit that like all football fans I want to watch my team win. I admit that challenges by Shrewsbury players almost invariably look fair to me. But I am not blind, stupid, cynical, nor unjust. What I want to see are keenly contested matches, games decided through football, not on the whim of some incompetent official. Is it impossible to find forty-odd good quality referees from the whole of England and to send them out with appropriate messages about running games in the right spirit?

After all this ranting, a poetic interlude.... The following quotation from William Wordsworth was on the sachet of sugar that I poured into my cup of coffee at the buffet:

...with an eye made quiet by the power
Of harmony, and the deep power of joy,
We see into the life of things.

– He must surely have just come from a Third Division football game and recollected it in a moment of tranquillity.

As it is the first home game of the season, I go to get my Membership card, or "Guarantee Card" as they now appear to call it. I have a collection of these at home dating from 1988 to the present, which for some reason I have not thrown out. The one absence in this sequence, and a significant one, is 1995-6. Mostly these cards have no benefit or function (except perhaps that they generate a trifling amount of money and provide a database of fans). There was a time (in the days of Maggie Thatcher) when membership cards were seen as a solution to crowd misbehaviour. Now the stewards don't even check membership cards on entry to the ground or, as they used to, when you go to the Riverside. The chief reason for acquiring a card is not the 5% discount at the Club Shop or free admission to Reserve Games, it is that it gives some sort of guarantee of a ticket for an all ticket game. Most years this would not matter much. However, the year you don't bother to acquire one, that is the year we draw Liverpool in the Cup and despite being a regular fan you cannot get a ticket whatever extremes you are prepared to go to. I wasn't the only one caught out like that. There were some who had not missed a game home or away all season who were not allowed a ticket. – As if supporting Shrewsbury Town were not difficult enough.

Crowd witticism of the day (from the stage of the game when certain elements of the crowd were happy just to bait the opposing fans – that is, before their wrath towards the match officials consumed them entirely): "Back to school soon!"

So; two games played. Won one. Lost one. Does this foretell mid-table obscurity come the end of the season? To give the *Shropshire Star* its due, the report by Lee McLaughlan was pretty accurate both as to the fact and the spirit of the afternoon. Let's keep the target for the next game simple: finish the game with eleven men.

Nick Hornby? What a whinger! Gets depressed when Arsenal don't win anything. He should try supporting a team that isn't always going to finish second to Manchester United, that mostly bumps along in the nether regions of the League and gets excited to win through to the second round of the FA Cup or to avoid being dumped into the Conference.

Tuesday 21st saw us removed from the Worthington Cup by Tranmere Rovers. I am fated this year to see no cup football involving Salop and the club will not progress beyond the first round in any competition. Jemson scored the consolation goal. He was also to score the winning goal on Saturday against Oxford United, one of his former teams.

All-time Salop Favourites Number One – Arthur Rowley

"You don't score sixty-four goals in eighty-six games at the highest level without being able to score goals." – Alan Green

First down on a team-sheet of all-time favourite Shrewsbury Town players has got to be **Arthur Rowley** (though my squad is actually being named according to the order of their dates of birth). He is the only one of those I have selected that I never saw play, but as a boy I followed his exploits closely. It was Roy of the Rovers stuff, though, unlike Roy's, Arthur's deeds were real enough and a good deal grittier, covered in mud and soaked in sweat.

Arthur Rowley (or G. Arthur Rowley to distinguish him from his namesake who played for Liverpool, Wrexham and Crewe in the 1950s, and from my wife's grandad also of the same name) was born in Wolverhampton in April 1926, younger brother of Albert (who played for Notts County) and Jack who was himself no slouch when it came to goal-scoring (netting an average of more than a goal every two games in his 317 post-War appearances for Manchester United). Their father Mark had been a semi-professional goalkeeper.

Arthur, as any schoolboy worth his trainers knows, holds the record for the number of goals scored in the Football League (434 or 433 as different sources maintain), and that in a career delayed a year or two by the War. During the War he was on amateur terms with Manchester United, for whom he made some 5 first team appearances (scoring once), including his debut against Liverpool at the age of 15. He also made several guest appearances for Wolves (scoring three times), but signed for West Bromwich Albion in March 1944 and played half a dozen games before being called up when 18. While in the army he continued to play for West Brom on occasion (his War-time tally with them was 9 goals in 16 appearances) and also guested for Brighton 5 times. He started his post-War career with West Bromwich Albion upon his demob. His time there was scarcely a sign of what was to happen later: he scored a mere 4 goals in 24 appearances. He then moved to Fulham in December 1948, scoring a respectable 27 goals (some sources give only 26) in 56 games (including 19 in a 22-match run) and helping them gain promotion to the First Division. His subsequent period at Leicester City, from 1950 to 1958, is legendary and almost impossible for modern football folk to believe. Here, booting around a heavy leather ball that would not at all suit those who like to bend their shots, he scored an amazing 251 goals in 303 appearances, including an amazing 44 goals in 42 appearances in 1956-7. Even the phenomenal Jimmy Greaves didn't quite match that strike-rate.

And of course Arthur did not finish there. Even in his thirties he continued to score regularly for Shrewsbury Town. Between 1958 and 1964 there were 152 goals in 236 League games, 11 goals in 19 FA Cup games, and 4 goals in 12 League Cup games.

At the age of 39 he finally gave up playing, reluctantly one feels, and concentrated on being a manager. The Club had prospered under his guidance and become established in the Third Division, narrowly missing promotion to the Second Division in 1968. He moved on to manage Sheffield United and Southend United, before returning to Shropshire for various roles with Telford United and Oswestry Town.

He was not only a footballer but also a cricketer, playing for Leicestershire Seconds and Shropshire. He was a leg-break bowler and batted at number 5 for Shropshire.

His record in football is truly exceptional by any standards and speaks for itself. Why such a prolific scorer never played for England is scarcely credible, particularly when you take into account the number of so called strikers who have had that honour without causing foreign goalkeepers to bend their backs. Arthur's only representative games were for England "B" and a Football League XI, which somehow do not have the same cachet. How they can justify not giving him a mention in the Queen's Honours List I likewise do not understand (though his omission probably says more about the way that arcane system operates than it does about Arthur's merits). He may not be a current sportsman, but there should be some recognition of lifetime's achievement.

The Arthur Interview

"I don't think that record will ever be broken or beaten." – Gerry Armstrong

I went to interview Arthur Rowley on the 22nd November 2002. I was greeted at the door with a handshake and "Hello. I'm Arthur." Arthur Rowley at 76 came across as a quietly spoken gentleman, not quick on his feet but still apparently in remarkably good shape for a man of his age. He was not garrulous but was quite willing to speak about most things (with the exception of his time at Sheffield United, which he obviously regretted). He was clearly someone who had looked after himself, a fact that his face testified to, bearing neither the ruddy ravages of drink nor even wrinkles. It was a great shock to me that he died almost a month to the day after my visit.

Arthur took great pride in what he achieved as a player and what he did for Shrewsbury Town. He loved playing football, particularly scoring goals, and would not have hesitated to do it all again if he had the chance. All those goals may have merged together in the memory, but the fact of that grand total and the manner of its accrual can never be taken away from him. His love of Shrewsbury and its people was evident in his return to settle here.

ALAN: Do you remember many of your goals vividly?

ARTHUR: Not really. You get so many so quickly you forget a lot about them.

ALAN: Was that something you really enjoyed?

ARTHUR: Scoring goals? Yes.

ALAN: Was it more enjoyable than actually playing football?

ARTHUR: No. It was more enjoyable when you scored goals. It was great playing football but then if you scored goals it made it even better.

ALAN: What was your greatest achievement in football?

ARTHUR: Taking Shrewsbury out of the one division into the next one.

ALAN: Do you regret that you just missed that next step up?

ARTHUR: We just missed out. – Yes I do, because it would have been great for the town. That was what I was interested in because we like it here and they're decent people. They're very good supporters really.

ALAN: You always got on well with the fans in Shrewsbury?

ARTHUR: Oh yes. Except when we lost. [He laughs.]

ALAN: Are there any particular matches that you remember with warm feelings?

ARTHUR: I think the Chelsea one. We went down there in the Fifth Round of the Cup and gave them a good game.

ALAN: Who did you most enjoy playing alongside?

ARTHUR: Derek Hines. We'd played together at Leicester and had got a good understanding.

ALAN: Did you ever play with Stanley Matthews?

ARTHUR: Yes. He used to say, "Give me the ball. Get the ball to me." That's all Stan could say: "Give me the ball." When we played for different teams we used to travel down by the same train. Then we played for the England Football League and so forth. He was a nice fellow, Stan. I like Stanley Matthews. There was no airs and graces about him; down to earth. Tom Finney was the best player I played with.

ALAN: You must have played against him a few times…

ARTHUR: Yes. Whatever you did to try and stop him, he'd still wriggle through. I think he was a better player than Matthews.

ALAN: Neither of them were very big, were they?

ARTHUR: No. Stanley was bigger, but I think Tommy was stronger.

ALAN: What about opponents? Was there any particular player you came up against that you found a bit of a challenge?

ARTHUR: Tommy Docherty. He was a case.

ALAN: Who was the best defender you came up against?

ARTHUR: John Harris – played for Chelsea.

ALAN: Was he skilful, or strong…?

ARTHUR: He was everything really. I had one or two tussles with Stan Cullis. He was a good player.

ALAN: How did you find it when you were player-manager? Was it difficult to do the two rôles?

ARTHUR: Not really. I enjoyed it; because you were not only with the players in the week but on the match day as well, which made it a bit easier because what you'd been doing in the week you could more or less put it right on the pitch if it wasn't going right. – Whereas if you were outside it wasn't quite as easy.

ALAN: And did being part of the team allow you to see the players' strengths and so on?

ARTHUR: Yes. You could see that in training as well. In playing you could see whether what we'd been trying to teach in training was going on on the field, because you're a lot closer.

ALAN: Which did you enjoy most, the playing or the managing?

ARTHUR: Playing.

ALAN: Was it your policy to have a number of key people with good football brains so you could rely on the fact that they were thinking?

ARTHUR: Well yes. That is what it's all about. You need four or five players to carry the other six along, and that improves their game because they've got somebody to help them. I mean, if they're all the same standard then you're just getting a wash all the while, but if someone's better than the others they can pull the others along. They can copy them and improve themselves. I mean, Peter Broadbent improved a lot of people down here with his play. I would think he was the best thing that ever happened down here when I brought him here.

ALAN: Did you find it a big difference coming to Shrewsbury to play, after being with teams like Leicester and West Brom?

ARTHUR: It was a bit different from Fulham. No – it didn't make any difference to me. I just went on the field to play football. I wasn't worried about what was going on outside. I enjoyed playing at Fulham. That was a nice club. Tommy Trinder used to keep you happy.

ALAN: He'd come into the changing rooms and cheer up the troops?

ARTHUR: Yes. Nice fellow, Tommy Trinder. Nice ground, right by the river. Fulham was one of the best pitches in the country then.

ALAN: How did you get into football? – Was it a family thing?

ARTHUR: Yes. My brother Jack played for England and Albert my other brother was a professional. He might have been the best but had a cartilage injury. At the back of the house we had a field and I used to be on there nearly every night; and my brother used to come and teach me. We weren't jealous of one another. We just got on.

ALAN: Did you regret not playing for England?

ARTHUR: I did because I thought I deserved to. I was top goalscorer and I thought I might get a chance. I played for the England B and the Football League and thought that was a stepping stone, but it never materialised. Perhaps if I'd stopped at Fulham I might have got in.

ALAN: Did you feel lucky to be a footballer?

ARTHUR: I was glad. I don't think I was lucky because I put a lot into it. It was a great life when I played and I'm glad I did it. I don't think I'd have changed it if I'd had the chance.

ALAN: Who in the game did you most respect?

ARTHUR: John Carey. I thought he was a great player. When we used to play against Manchester United, he used to stand out. There were quite a few, but he's the one who springs to mind.

ALAN: Did you find it difficult to make the transition from football to life-after-football?

ARTHUR: You do. You miss it – because it's not a full time job is it, football, then? Then you get a job and you're starting at 8 or 7 in the morning and then you know that's the difference. But you get used to it. You've got to earn a living somehow.

ALAN: I suppose what you did eased you out anyway. You went from playing to player-manager to manager.

ARTHUR: Yes. I did a bit in the local leagues for different people. I went to Telford. I ran their second team for a bit, the Juniors – got them going. We did quite well. Used to keep my hand in.

ALAN: Has football changed much since your day?

ARTHUR: Yes. It's not the same. It's not allowed to flow now like it used to.

ALAN: Was that to do with changes to rules or…?

ARTHUR: Where you used to be able to tackle and so forth, it looks as though that's gone out of the game. This is what I think the difference is.

ALAN: Do you think you'd like to play in the 21st Century or did you prefer it in your day?

ARTHUR: If I were younger I'd like to be playing any time, because it was my life.

ALAN: Would you like to play the game as it is now or as it was?

ARTHUR: I prefer it as it was, but I'd still like to play it again now.

ALAN: Would you encourage a son or nephew to become a professional footballer now?

ARTHUR: Oh yes. We did have one, but unfortunately it didn't turn out.

ALAN: Do you think that's better for him?

ARTHUR: I think so because he's got a good job now. I never pushed him. I think if you push them it's wrong. They should decide what they want to do themselves.

ALAN: What do you think of the amount of money footballers get paid these days?

ARTHUR: What do you think, ducks? [To his wife who has just entered the room.]

Mrs Rowley: £12 a week we used to get. £2 for a win and a pound for a draw. Now they have millions, don't they?

ARTHUR: Well good luck to them, I say. If the clubs are daft enough to pay it.

Mrs Rowley: I feel sorry for the little clubs though, those that can't afford to splash out like that.

ALAN: Do you watch much football nowadays?

ARTHUR: Yes. I go to Shrewsbury quite a few times.

ALAN: Who did you grow up following?

ARTHUR: Wolves. It wasn't far away. I used to train down there when Billy Wright and all those were there. And Major Buckley.

ALAN: What do you think of this possible move from the Gay Meadow?

ARTHUR: They were on about it when I was here before! I think it's got to happen. They can't expand, that's the trouble. It's difficult on a match day to get in.

ALAN: 434. I don't see anybody beating that.

ARTHUR: If they did I'd be the first to congratulate them, because I think in these days it'd be a great achievement, greater than mine.

(This interview appeared in the *Shropshire Star* on Saturday 21st December, 2002.)

Tuesday 28th August, 2001
"I would also think that the action replay showed it to be worse than it actually was." – Ron Atkinson

York City (home) ; Football League Division Three

Previous record in league games:					
Home			Away		
Win	Draw	Lose	Win	Draw	Lose
9	2	3	5	3	6

3-2 (HT 1-0); Rodgers (9), Jagielka (66), Jemson (89)
Attendance: 3,002
Standpoint: On the Riverside, just in front of the band (or at least where they would have been if they'd been there).

My chief memory of York City does not actually feature Shrewsbury. A couple of years ago York were the victims of a giant-killing act by Hednesford Town and I was there to witness Tim Clarke (formerly of the Town, in the mid-nineties) beaten on that day. When I say I was there, I wasn't actually inside the ground. The capacity of the Hednesford ground was already well and truly exceeded by the time I arrived, but the bloke on the turnstiles helpfully informed me that I could stand on the embankment at the side of the ground. It looked like a left-over from mining days but it may as well have been purpose built. Along with several hundred others I had an excellent view of a game that the non-League team deserved to win. Incidentally, the Hednesford team that night included, I recall, Kevin Collins (who played one game for Salop in 1984) and the near legendary Bernard McNally.

The anticipation is great once more after another Jemson goal brought the second Town away League victory in a row. When was the last time we started the season with two away victories? (The answer to that semi-rhetorical and wholly ridiculous question is of course 1996, when we defeated Rotherham and Burnley in our first two away encounters of the season, though we had started the campaign with a drawn home game.) A pleasing comparison might also be made to the years when we have struggled for any away wins. We also met my modest target of finishing the game with eleven players on the pitch. This time it had been Oxford United's turn to be numerically disadvantaged.

For the game Freestone kept his place. Murray was on the bench, but should get his chance when other suspensions kick in. He also apparently has other matters on his mind that will be well documented in the local press and I won't go into at the moment. I respect him as a footballer; affairs beyond that are not my business. He has a right to privacy, even when his actions off the football field bring him into the public arena.

Brilliant. Infuriating. Nail-biting. – A few of the adjectives applicable to Town's performance in tonight's match.

Presumably Nigel Jemson lost the toss because the teams changed ends before kick-off so that Town were attacking the goal at the Wakeman End which these days we normally do in the second-half. Salop began the game with some beautifully flowing passing movements. This phase culminated in a stupendous individual goal by Luke Rodgers, when he carried the ball at speed into the box and hit a scorcher from the left side. Unfortunately this was a signal for Town to sit back and soak up pressure for the rest of the half.

For the first quarter of an hour of the second-half the policy was similar, except that the containment was done largely in midfield. Then Sam Aiston was brought on and from his first run down the left wing he crossed the ball straight to the feet of Steve Jagielka. I probably would not have missed from there and nor did Jags. 2-0 and coasting, which almost proved costly. York scored a goal and for the first time in the game looked as though they believed they could get something. They were momentarily halted in their tracks by a magnificent turn and volley on the edge of the box by Nigel Jemson. When did the Town last score three such distinctive and brilliant goals in one game? Unfortunately they relaxed again and York hit a second. The last few minutes were, shall we say, anxious.

They say a 2-0 lead is dangerous, and I've seen a few games that have borne that out. Town showed themselves capable of some of the best team-work I've seen from them in recent years, but the foot can't be safely taken off the pedal until the game is completely wrapped up (six goals might do). If Mark Cartwright hadn't tipped a couple of shots over the bar, Town might have been embarrassed to find themselves losing a game they should have had under control.

Still, it all contributes to football as a spectacle, to football as the delightfully unpredictable.

I see in the matchday programme that Kevin Ratcliffe believes 99% of referees would not even have given a foul for the incident that led to Mark Atkins being sent off against Hartlepool. He also comments in connection with the question of whether the referee might change his decision after seeing the video evidence that "it takes a good man to admit to a mistake". That would make David Ellery a good man, because he has reversed his first red card decision in the Everton-Spurs game. Unfortunately Mr Redcard has not changed his mind concerning Mark Atkins. (Redcard is obviously not his real name, which may be on public record but will not be dignified with mention here.)

According to the *Shropshire Star*, Terry Dolan, the York City manager, believed that it was a perfectly good goal when they had the ball in the net just before half-time. Of course he would have had a first class view from the dug-out by the half-way line, but I had a better one. I was in line with play, as was the assistant referee, and I can assure Mr Dolan that the assistant referee was absolutely correct in this instance. It was off-side. In fact the officials got it right on a much higher percentage of decisions (not, for example, waving play on after a blatant hand-ball, Mr Redcard). Perhaps more importantly, even if the decisions weren't always spot-on, they were made firmly and with a soupçon of good humour but without any of the confrontational, macho posturing.

One hears such strange conversations at football matches, at Shrewsbury anyway.

"Those composers were a romantic lot."

"The Romantics certainly were. How d'you mean?"

"Well, Beethoven wrote that Für Elise."

"What's that?"

"For Elise. It was dedicated to some woman. Then there was Schubert."

"Is that the fizzy powder?"

"No, you fool. When he wrote his *Trout Quintet* he promised he would even die for Ella."

My sugar sachets these week feature Sir Isaac Newton, who as well as heading apples apparently also invented the mirror telescope, and Red Rum who was certainly a superstar and fit to have his image at any sporting occasion.

This win lifts Town to fifth in the table. That doesn't mean much at this early stage though, but it's an improvement on wondering where the next and/or first point is to come from. It also raises the profile of Saturday's game away to Bristol Rovers, who have also started well. We can head off to Bristol in good heart for what ought to be a cracking game. Town would have stood an excellent chance, except for the fact that this will be the game when Matt Redmile and Mark Atkins have to serve their suspensions. Potentially the actions of the man with the whistle who ruined the Hartlepool game and robbed Town of three points could well have their echo on Saturday. He may therefore prove to have cost the Town two games. However, we do have an able replacement centre-half in Andrew Tretton and there are one or two possibilities in midfield, including re-instating Karl Murray, if he is ready.

1st September

"They've got their feet on the ground and if they stay that way they'll go places." – John Gidman

What an unbelievable day! Not only did England turn in their most exciting performance since 1966 and arguably their most amazing result ever, but Mr Redcard's legacy did not cause Salop undue problems at Bristol Rovers. No goals scored for the first time this year in a competitive game; but none conceded either, so we maintain our promising start and useful league position. It might be premature to believe that England have now qualified for the World Cup Finals (or even won the World Cup according to some); there are still a couple of games to win. It is even more the case that it is too early to start getting excited about Town's promotion or play-off chances. Let's get on a bit further with the season, shall we?

Saturday 8th September, 2001
"If we played like this every week, we wouldn't be so inconsistent" – Bryan Robson

Cheltenham Town (home); Football League Division Three

Previous record in league games:					
Home			Away		
Win	Draw	Lose	Win	Draw	Lose
1	—	1	1	1	—

2-1 (HT 2-0); N.Jemson (20), L.Rodgers (39)
Attendance: 3395
Standpoint: For most of the game, on the Riverside, again leaning against a barrier just in front of where the band are supposed to be. (What has happened to them?)

This had better be good and not the exhausted, nail-biting anticlimax of England versus Albania. I have forgone an invitation to a wedding to be here.

Of course it was not good. In the same way that the England-Albania game was hard going after the euphoria of Germany-England, so after the recent promise this game against a team struggling to get its season started was always likely to be painful. Nevertheless, at the end of it the Town have moved to second in the table; and if it's true that the sign of a good team is to win when not playing well, then we are scheduled for promotion this year.

I got soaked on my way between the town and the ground. Then, perversely, there was glorious sunshine throughout the game. The Cheltenham line-up included the optimistically (but, as it turned out, erroneously) named Jamie Victory. My pleasure during the first half was diminished a little by being forced to secondary-smoke my neighbour's chain of cigarettes. Apart from pubs and kipper factories, football grounds are becoming one of the few places where this happens these days.

The members of the team are playing well as individuals. The effort and commitment are evident but there is little cohesion. They show they are capable of fluent passing movements, yet resort too often to high balls hit from the back that are gobbled up by the grateful opposition. The only bright spots were the two goals. The first followed an excellent piece of refereeing when the game was allowed to continue despite a foul. Nigel Jemson took full advantage. He jinked his way into the penalty area and turned the full-back inside out in a demonstration of nimble footwork that any dancer would envy, before smashing in a right-foot shot.

The referee, who had an excellent game, then went back and booked the offending full-back. This unfortunate young man did not have the best of afternoons, probably being a little rattled by elements in the crowd who firstly made remarks about his mother and followed that up with taunts about his sexuality. It is difficult, but the only worthwhile way to react to such unsporting behaviour is to ignore it and exact revenge through a brilliant performance.

Match officials sometimes have this problem too at the Meadow. They are hailed, often in a jovial fashion, by someone in the crowd. The mistake is to respond. The assistant referee's only hope is to act as if he is totally wrapped up in the game and has not heard any remarks addressed to him. Any sign that he is at all conscious of the crowd – is in any way human even – is taken for weakness. To so much as smile at some witticism has been the downfall of many a linesman, who thereafter has suffered a stream of abuse that would not be contemplated, let alone permitted, in any other circumstances in our society. Matters have improved with regard to the crowd's use of racist insults, but there is a way to go before perfection is reached in attitude and word.

The Town's second goal came from Luke Rodgers who was put through to outpace the defenders and rasp the ball past the goal-keeper, Carl Muggleton. The keeper managed to touch the ball but was very annoyed with himself when he failed to keep it out of the net. Someone near me remarked that Cheltenham have gone behind 2-0 in all of their games so far this season, whatever the final outcome. I don't know the truth of this, but it is possible. They certainly played with spirit and deserved better luck against a Town side who were content to sit on their lead. They undoubtedly deserved the goal they scored after a period of pressure in the second half and few Salop fans would really deny that, in light of the underperformance of our own team.

I know that there is hope of a new stadium [I originally wrote "soon", a word becoming less appropriate with each passing month], but there are signs that the current one is being let go somewhat. The score-box that had stood for years on the Wakeman End where it meets the Riverside terraces was demolished a couple of years ago and not replaced. Many stadia these days have electronic screens that give all sorts of instant information (even action replays). We have to make do with someone booming distortion and feedback over the Tannoy. The toilets at the far end of the ground have been shut since last year's floods. They were always on the primitive side – little more than pig troughs screened by corrugated sheets – but they represented a convenience of sorts. There is also evidence that nature is beginning to reclaim the terraces. Today I noticed just in front of me a small buddleia, a nettle and some plantain all climbing out of the crack between steps on the terrace. There was also some unnameable weed squeezing from between breeze blocks in the wall surrounding the pitch. These are perhaps the result of seeds carried here and fertilised by the floods, but they might need a dose of Weedol if we are to stand on the terraces without risking nettle-rash or being attacked by butterflies driven to a frenzy by the sight of a butterfly-plant. If the stadium suffers much more neglect it will begin to resemble my garden.

Some of the tunes appropriated by the fans for their terrace chants and songs are undoubtedly fitting. A good example is *The British Grenadier*, which might I suppose count as a battle song as well as suggesting pride for the cause; the Salop version includes the lines "From the banks of the River Severn / To the shores of Sicily, / We will fight, fight, fight for Shrewsb'ry, / Till we win Division Three".

Other tunes are wonderfully inappropriate. Today, for example the Cheltenham fans were being taunted with a couple of chants. There was "Back to the Conf'rence; you're going back to the Conf'rence"; pure derision sung to the tune of the exotic and evocative ditty *Guantanamera*. It may be Cuba's most famous song (and about an honest man from where palms grow who cultivates white roses in June as well as January), but it is one of the all-purpose tunes for the football crooner. There was also "Next year – you're playing Telford next year", to the tune of the romantic *Blue Moon*. Another favourite is the "Feed me till I want no more" line from *Bread of Heaven*; this hymn tune is wonderfully versatile and adapts to lines such as "Can we play you ev'ry week?" and "Did you think you'd scored a goal?". Although the original lyric is not a question, all of the lines sung to this tune seem to be interrogatives, possibly because of the way the intonation rises perceptibly at the end. Another popular religious tune, *Lord of the Dance*, is used for the delightfully inappropriate lyrics "Fight, fight, wherever you may be, / We are the boys of Shrewsbury." Are these incongruities between form and subject matter deliberate, or is the irony unintentional?

Equally laden with irony has been the use of the pop songs *Catch Us If You Can* and *Simply the Best* to introduce the team at the start of games. There have been times in the history of the club when far from stirring the home team to greater heroics these songs must have sounded like someone telling jokes at a funeral service, or like another kick up the backside. It is difficult to feel urged to action even by Tina Turner's rousing chorus when you are the bottom team in the Football League and know that the words are complete nonsense.

My remarks about the crowd's baiting of the players, officials and rival fans might make the Meadow seem an unfriendly place. It is far from that. The only reason such behaviour has any effect is that the ground is relatively intimate. A player might find the crowd at Old Trafford or Anfield much more intimidating as a mass, but how conscious are they of individuals within that crowd?

The Meadow is actually a wonderfully unthreatening place to be. The only times when this has not been the case have been when visiting fans have come in great numbers and with some sense of unease or dread, usually for the last game of a season. A prime example of this was when West Bromwich Albion came in May 1992. They were possibly frustrated at the prospect of another season in the Third Division (though it was Town who were to be relegated further) and at the end of the game not only invaded the pitch but caused damage to the goals that Attila the Hun would have had difficulty in emulating. This, however, was nothing in comparison to the visit of Middlesbrough in 1986. Town won that day, which pushed Middlesbrough into the Third Division (I think it was for the first time in their history) and even threatened the existence of the club. The visiting supporters were so pleased by the result that the scene was very ugly. Town fans were kept in the ground while their guests were dispersed. We weren't too chuffed by that and they weren't too inclined to be co-operative with police and stewards. When I eventually emerged, I found that my wife who had been waiting for me outside the ground was very distressed, as much by the slavering police-dogs that seemed not to like her as by the mass of vicious humanity that had been sweeping past in imitation of Attila's armies.

These are quieter days. Now there tend to be few visiting fans for League games, there being currently a shortage of slumbering giants in the Third Division. The friendliness of the place is also evidenced by small touches like the physio, Simon Shakeshaft, coming off the pitch after treating a player and dispensing lollipops to youngsters standing against the wall at the front of the crowd. Would that happen at Old Trafford?

They also try to create a friendly atmosphere before games and during the intervals. Lenny the Lion dishes out sweets (often at his own expense, the generous man) and cavorts about the pitch when the players are warming up. At half time, after the draws for the "Golden Gamble" and the Family Stand, they attempt entertainment from time to time. The last couple of games have seen the Up Town Girls (clever name, eh?) prancing about to pre-recorded music like cheer-leading pom-pom dancers or drum-majorettes. To my taste, that might be fine as a one-off. I prefer the military bands that visit occasionally, or, even better, the American-style shoot-outs that Dick Pratley used to organise for the youngsters. Those had at least some connection to football and gave little kids the opportunity to tread the hallowed turf and attempt to show their dribbling and shooting skills.

My sugar this week came wrapped in images of the Crystal Palace (which, if only for its name, does have relevance to English football, I suppose) and the Empire State Building. I have actually stood on the viewing gallery of this New York building a couple of times, which is particularly poignant at the point I am writing up my notes based on the Cheltenham Town game. Between the game and now has fallen 11th September, a date that will be forever linked with the destruction of the Empire State's near neighbouring twin towers of the World Trade Center. That fact and all the attendant circumstances puts into proper perspective much of what we do on this earth. Whatever the result of Salop's game at Mansfield this coming Friday, it will certainly have a reduced significance in the light of this week's events.

What happened in America was born of hatred and complete disregard of the sanctity of life. To my mind there is a relevance in this to the world of football. How many football fans regularly chant: "We hate [supply name of nearest rivals]"? How many of the supporters uttering these words do so with any understanding or conviction? If both understanding and conviction are involved, this strikes me as out of proportion and potentially dangerous. Football is a game. For a Shrewsbury supporter to claim to hate Telford fans is a nonsense. They are not only fellow Salopians but fellow human beings. We should support our own team with passion, but restrict comments against supporters of other teams to light-hearted fun. Likewise when in fanzines local rivals are verbally and scatologically abused this strikes me as either poor humour, poor taste or plain misguidedness. How can a country claim to be civilised when identifying with eleven men kicking a pig's bladder leads to venomous speech or action and civil war masquerades as club loyalty? Football should be a substitute for war, not the cause of enmity and hatred.

– Not long after I wrote the preceding paragraph one of the East Anglian teams had to apologise for its scoreboard referring to its local rivals as “the Scum”.

All-time Salop Favourites Number Two – Peter Dolby

“He’s working hard. One moment he’s on the left, the next moment he’s on the right. At the moment he’s in the middle.” – Ron Jones

Peter Dolby was that rare breed, a one-club man (if we discount the non-league starting-points of Derby Corinthians and Heanor Town and his sneaking off, as he puts it, “to play for Crewe Alexandra in the famous, but long-forgotten, Watney Cup competition against Carlisle United at Gresty Road in the company of Stanley Bowles”). He was born in Derby in May 1940 and signed for Salop in February 1960, after scoring against Brentford on his debut in January. He was initially only part-time, as he was completing an apprenticeship with Rolls Royce. He signed full-time in October 1961. In a playing career that continued until 1975 he played 303 league games (plus 21 as sub), scoring 21 times. He also played 31 games (plus one as sub) in the F.A. Cup (4 goals) and 15 times in the League Cup (4 goals).

In his early games he tended to play as an inside forward and had a creditable strike rate (5 goals in 8 outing in his first part-season). He soon became a regular at centre-half, though there were still times in his career when he was pushed into a more attacking role, including several games as number 9, and he would doubtless have scored many more goals had he been deployed up front more frequently. His appearances became rarer during the 1970s and he played his final game when he came on as sub against Walsall on September 22nd 1975.

It is two of his goals in the League Cup that particularly earn him a place in Meadow mythology. The memory of how in the very first year of the League Cup (1960-1) Salop defeated mighty Everton with two goals from Dolby may now be a distant one but it is nonetheless precious. For a club like Shrewsbury Town such moments do not come very often, so they are particularly treasured when they do. A player who makes the telling contribution to such an occasion is bound to be honoured in the Club’s communal memory. Indeed, his spectacular feat against Everton throws slightly into the shade cup goals against two other footballing giants, Manchester City (January 1965) and Arsenal (January 1968). He was truly a goalscorer for the big occasion. He claims all his goals were important, even the own goal he scored when Salop were playing Carlisle in their epic Cup battle of 1966.

The image with which I associate Peter Dolby in my mind is that of a flamingo – strange, I know, and in many ways scarcely appropriate, but it captures for me that slender grace possessed by a creature that should be all gangling legs and pointy knees. It is also an image that is somehow in keeping with the affable gentlemanly side of his nature (remarkably for a centre-half he was booked by a referee only once). The main reasons it is not an entirely suitable association is that a flamingo would be neither a powerful header of a ball nor a hard tackler, and any footballer who plays the bulk of his career as a centre half (and who also happens to be the son of a boxer) has, at least on the football pitch, a steel in his character that a pink-feathered bird would probably not possess.

I should point out that he himself does not much like this comparison, preferring a description first bestowed by a rival fan. Apparently a Millwall supporter once screamed out as Dolby headed the ball away: "Get that f——— giraffe out of the penalty area!" Peter Dolby comments: "Quite an apt description I always felt and one that the late Stan Hall of the Shrewsbury Chronicle, a fine pen-man, agreed with, pointing out that the rather loping run and those gangly legs you mention only added to the likeness. My ability to slip, trip and fall over invisible objects on the pitch brought the name of one of Walt Disney's characters to the fore in my early days, along with that of 'mobile television aerial' (the old H variety I presume)."

After his playing days were over Peter Dolby maintained his links with the Club by coaching the youth and junior teams on a part time basis.

The Wap Interview

"Who's shit on the floor?" "Me, Boss, but I'm not bad in the air." – A probably apocryphal exchange between Bill Shankly and Tony

Hateley, when the former asked about the deposit made on the floor by the club cat.

In case the title of this section is a little obscure, the nickname "Wap" was bestowed upon Peter Dolby by full-back Gordon Skeech, because of his ability to strike the ball hard – to "wap" it. This ability may have impressed his fellow footballers, but I was just as impressed with the fact that he knew this was onomatopoeia (and what's more he could spell it). I've met English teachers who couldn't do that, never mind footballers.

During the writing of this book I spent an entire day in his entertaining and informative company. Unlike the stereotypical footballer, Peter can be fairly described as articulate. He has an inexhaustible supply of anecdotes about football, life and Shrewsbury Town. I learnt from him an amazing amount of background to the Shrewsbury Town story, a great deal being of the sort that is not readily apparent or accessible to even the most ardent fan. A large part of what he told me I do not intend to recount here. Apart from material that would class as confidential, there is much that is already in the public domain (such as his part in the Everton, Manchester City and Arsenal games) and a significant amount that he would tell better himself in the book that he should (and just might) write – such as how he was expelled from school; or the time when he was ousted from his hotel room in Prague by the Harlem Globetrotters; or how he talked the Chairman into buying the team suits for the visit to play Chelsea in the Cup; or the pit-falls of public-speaking.

A football match is an event involving many people, all of whom could be described as participants in some sense (even the person watching the game on a TV screen is a participant in the event). I am writing this book from the perspective of the fan – the engaged spectator – and as such was interested to explore the relationship between my memories of former games and what memories a player might have. Some people no doubt have complete recall, but as a fan who has watched several hundred Shrewsbury Town games I am often hazy about detail, some games merge in the mind, some have vanished into oblivion. What is it like for the player, who has been actively involved – in over four hundred Salop games in the case of Peter Dolby? Is his recall similarly selective? Do the bulk of games become one amorphous mass in the memory? As it turns out Peter Dolby's memory is quite remarkable (how representative this is, I'm not sure). His recall of games is impressive. Some of the names may elude him now but he can often tell what happened on the field and what was going on behind the scenes. This is largely because football has been his life and he has been fully wrapped up in it.

Peter Dolby was a grammar school boy who always wanted to be a footballer. He could have followed his father into boxing but saw football as a less brutal option. As a child he was surrounded by his father's sporting friends (including the legendary Raich Carter, who was playing for Derby County at the time). Being struck down with rheumatic fever as a teenager may have raised doubts in the minds of doctors and deprived him of the opportunity to represent his school at the top level but merely served to strengthen his resolve. He played for local sides Derby Corinthians (for whom he hit a rich vein of goalscoring, including a couple of hat-tricks past future team-mate Mike Gibson) and Heanor Town (from where Nigel Pearson would also come to Salop). When the chance of higher grade football came along he opted for Salop ahead of West Ham (his father didn't want him going to London), Mansfield Town and Headington United (the future Oxford United). His father, no doubt very wisely, insisted that he see out his engineering apprenticeship and he was still working at Rolls Royce when he hit the headlines with his two goals against Everton.

When he joined Salop Peter Dolby recommended his friend and later best man Mike Gibson (then playing at Nuneaton Borough), who was duly signed a month later. That was the start of another aspect of his services to the club. Years later, as senior pro, he was often assigned the job of talking to promising players and assist in persuading them to sign for the club. Such players included Graham Turner and Paul Maguire. Later still he played a large part in bringing players such as Dave Linighan and Nigel Pearson to the club.

Peter Dolby's relationship with Salop fans has always been an easy one, partly because he knew how to react to the crowd and also because he saw it as an obligation to give them his best – as he puts it: "If you've paid your whatever it was in those days, I think you're entitled to my best efforts for the full ninety minutes every time and I always endeavoured to do that for you." He has a definite sense that he is lucky to have had the opportunity of a career in football. Another factor in his relationship with the fans is that he has lived among them for many years. In addition, as a young semi-professional footballer, he worked alongside the local people, many of whom were ardent Salop fans. Some fellow workers at Rolls Royce, however, were also quite capable of inflicting jibes and taunts when things hadn't gone well – such as the wags who pinned up on the notice-board: "Up the line the train came chuffin'; Reading five, Shrewsbury nuffin'." His response to this would have been one of good humour. In any case all negatives would have been eclipsed for him by the vivid memory of the amazing response as he walked in the morning after the Everton game. All his work-mates stood at their machines and greeted him with a symphony of spanners on metal. In his own words: "It doesn't get any better than that." That may have been the high-spot but it set the scene for a long-term rapport. Even now as he walks to the ground he will be customarily hailed with the unoriginal "Got your boots, Dolb?" and the like.

Peter Dolby comes across not only as an honest professional, but one with a shrewd football brain (developed by qualifying as an FA coach whilst a player and honed by constant use), capable of influencing a game by analysing a situation and recognising what would be needed to turn matters in Salop's favour. As a player, he says, "After twenty minutes I'll tell you all about the centre-forward. Is he left-footed? Is he right-footed? Is he quick? Is he very quick? Is he good in the air? Is he very brave? Because I've tried all those things out." He counts himself as having been a "psychologically good" player who could "recognise what you're against" and had "an awareness of what's going on". He can point to games where he made a difference by suggesting some tactical ploy, such as employing George Boardman's ability as a man-marker in a big cup tie away at Millwall (January 1965). This influence endured beyond his playing days, when he used to be involved in the pre-match work and sorting out the game plan; for example, he advised that the only way to deal with Ipswich's brilliant Dutch midfielder Arnold Muhren in the 1982 FA Cup was to ensure that our midfield did not get drawn too far forward, but instead hang on to the ball, keep tight and virtually mark Muhren man-for-man. As a result we won the game 2-1 (with goals from Steve Cross and Jake King).

He contends that part of Arthur Rowley's managerial policy was to have a number of key people with good football brains (such as Ted Hemsley, Trevor Meredith, Peter Broadbent and himself). In the side this may have compensated for the lack of sophistication in training techniques (which in those days consisted largely of running) and some tactical planning. Peter Dolby confirms that as a young player he picked things up as he went along rather than being systematically coached. Thus he was introduced to "wall pass", a fairly basic coaching term, a long time after understanding and practising the move, and he recalls the painful lesson that experience taught him when he underestimated Mark Lazarus's speed and was caught out trying to be over elaborate himself. He was grateful to trainer Tommy Seymour for pointing out that he needed to keep his eyes open to the moment of contact when heading the ball; that simple advice made a big impact on his heading ability. Generally, however, in the days before coaching developed it was down to the player to decide why he hadn't played so well.

Harry Gregg introduced weights to the training regime. This didn't suit Peter whose physique does not rely on body-building. On being urged by Harry to put more effort into the weights Peter once retorted: "My insides'll be coming out of my arse, Boss, if I lift any more."

There were confrontations between the two of them concerning how the game should be played from both a coaching and physical approach, but he found Harry Gregg rather Jekyll and Hyde. Gregg was generally a tough disciplinarian, so the worse was to be expected when he called Peter into his office one day. The previous day Peter had excused himself from pre-season training, saying he was "completely knackered" and was going off home to sleep. Instead of reading the riot act, however, Harry greeted him with: "Very good, very professional. You're a bit older now. That's using your common-sense. Don't make a habit of it. But I understand." Peter Dolby was shrewd enough of course to tell his fellow players that he had been given a severe roasting.

He had first met Harry Gregg when they played together in a testimonial match at the Bucks Head shortly before Gregg became the Town manager. Gregg had been very affable and informed the back five that anything in the penalty area was his. True to his word he then dealt with everything authoritatively. Conversely Ken Mulhearn claimed that he'd get a nose-bleed if he were to come anywhere out of the six-yard box. He was nevertheless a fine goalkeeper and a great shot-stopper. However, in Peter Dolby's estimation the best keeper he played with was Alan Boswell, alongside his lifelong friend Mike Gibson.

Another incident that Peter Dolby recalls during Harry Gregg's reign occurred in September 1969, a few months after Gerry Bridgwood had joined Salop. "GB – What a star! A bit like having Norman Wisdom on the right wing. – Bouncy and full of cheek. What a good player; do tricks for fun; he'd come from Stoke and he was good." Bridgwood was rooming with Peter Dolby after Salop had played a League game at Fulham and prior to a League Cup game at Southend. He insisted that he was going out into Ascot for the evening, which put Peter Dolby into the position of having to go with him to make sure he kept out of trouble. After some difficulty in prising him away from the bright lights of Ascot and the minor problem of getting a taxi that would take them back to their hotel (GB managed this by claiming they were well-known Stoke City players), they eventually arrived back in the early hours of the morning only to find the doors locked. The door-man let them in but they then had another slight obstacle to negotiate in the form of Harry Gregg, the club chairman and Maurice Evans, who were still at the bar. Maurice Evans ("what a diamond bloke!") saved their bacon by distracting the other two while Messrs Dolby and Bridgwood crept past.

Alan Durban brought with him the wisdom, psychology and games-playing learnt from hundreds of games, thirty odd internationals and Cloughie. He introduced "patterns of play". It was

Durban who directed that defenders should not indulge in fancy work with the ball: "If I wanted a ball-player I'd buy a seal." Quite a few of Peter Dolby's later appearances for Town were as substitute, often replacing Alan Durban for the last 15 to 20 minutes and being instructed to "keep it going" – something in the nature of a no-win situation.

Peter Dolby maintains that he was well looked after by the Club in terms of such things as being taken to stay in good hotels (although there is an embarrassing incident that he will recount in his book about Alan Boswell asking for an extra egg). He did, like many players then, play a number of games at the end of a season when he was carrying an injury, which was probably not uncommon in football generally at the time. The standard of the Club's laundry arrangements also seem less than perfect, not to say somewhat primitive, with all kit being washed only once a week and hung in the coke-fired boiler room. It was first-come first gets the decent and drier kit on training days. He remembers the great Peter Broadbent arriving last one winter's day, picking up disdainfully the pitiful looking and scorched shirt that was left for him and remarking: "Seven caps for England and I have to wear this."

The other players may have been somewhat embarrassed that Peter Broadbent should be the one to draw the shortest straw in terms of respectable kit, but, having no airs and graces about him, he nevertheless wore the offending items. Peter Dolby talks of the sensation of rooming with someone who had formerly been something of a hero as being indescribable and certainly incapable of appreciation by anyone else. Broadbent was probably held in some awe by the other players but had a quiet modesty. On one occasion, for example, on a long journey home players were comparing the largest crowds they had played before. Peter Broadbent proffered nothing until asked directly, "What's the biggest crowd you played in front of?" He replied almost casually: "Probably be the Maracana – two hundred and ten thousand." (Possibly an exaggeration, though crowd figures at the Maracana were not scientifically accurate in the fifties when Peter Broadbent played for England against Brasil.)

There was to be no winding down for Peter Dolby after the playing stopped. He continued his Salop and football connection in the form of coaching and scouting, whilst doing a full-time teaching job and running a newsagents. He almost made a lot of money when offered the chance to join Jimmy Hill's band of coaches going out to Saudi Arabia, but stayed in England for mainly family reasons. He did go abroad briefly to play in the United States when "soccer" was growing there. He also acted as go-between for other players, including Tony Hateley and Graham French, fixing them up to play for the Boston Minutemen in the States. He blames the greed of certain European players for the decline of this early American venture into football.

His phenomenal work ethic has eased a little now he is in his sixties, but he still retains his enthusiasm for football and coaches youngsters at various levels. He also keeps his brain active with crosswords and reading rather than dulling it with too much television.

PD on PD

I don't think I was ever physically big enough to capture people's serious attention. I think most people who came to watch me said, "Bloody hell – how does he do that?" And I accept that. I weighed ten stones six when I was playing. I was always probably a stone light of playing at the top level. However, I've played against many top strikers, but can honestly say no top player's run me ragged.

PD on Arthur

Arthur – a remarkable man, to whom I owe a lot. I feel that at some stage Arthur decided I was the sort of person he could trust to some extent. I think he felt my contribution to the team was quite large really in terms of as well as what I did from the playing point of view – you know, this ability to organise players and do all that sort of thing.

I remember the first game I played for Shrewsbury. It was a charity game against Wrexham and we were a goal down. There was a free kick. Arthur puts the ball down, a great wall of red-shirted Wrexham lads in front of him. He just lay back and crashes the ball through them – nearly took the net out.

Against Grimsby a ball drops to him on the half-way line, he just looks towards goal, and he lays back and hits it with his left foot. He blasts it in. It catches the wind – he's allowed for that – and it just goes. The keeper just can't believe it.

He was a remarkable, remarkable player. He played in the old inside-left position for most of the time I played with him. He'd got this ability to – because we played with wingers then – this ability to sweep the ball out wide to get the right winger in with a great ball from just over the half-way line. An early ball and then he would follow up because the play would get in front of him and then anything that came out of the box he would uncannily be in the right position to come onto them and often he'd just slam them in.

He was tremendous. The best contest I ever saw was with George Curtis on a mud-heap of a pitch at Coventry. A clash of two dinosaurs with Arthur coming out on top.

He's an interesting character. I'm surprised no-one's written a biography.

PD on Salop's Centre-Halves

I watched Dave Linighan play in an intermediate game at Derby and asked their trainer about him: "He's third or fourth in line here, Jack. He's got no chance." We bought him for buttons and the rest is history.

My brother Steve phoned me up from Derby one night. He said, "Heanor Town have got a centre-half better than you." — Nigel Pearson. I asked Ted Hemsley to check him out for us and he confirmed his ability. Ron Jukes, the chief scout, gets the credit for finding Nigel Pearson, but Ted and I played our parts.

Nigel and I have remained good friends. I played alongside big Jim Holton as well, which was lovely too as he went on to play for Manchester United and Scotland.

Nigel's probably the best of all the centre-halves I've seen, and along with Jackie Keay (1977-82) the most complete of the centre-halves. But we've had some tremendous centre-halves at this club. And I put myself in that list; I think I was a good centre-half. But we've had some greats. I mean: Colin Griffin. Totally reliable game after game if a bit short of flair, Colin; just a very good steady centre-half. But Nigel had just a bit of something more about him, didn't he, as he went on to show at Sheffield?

PD on the importance of working with youngsters

It's a long, slow, tortuous process to get the grass roots of football sorted.... Saturday morning I'll be coaching kids. 62 and out there putting posts up. I've been coaching and managing youngsters on a regular basis for thirty years at least, and I still love doing it, because I see the value of it for young people. It's got everything to offer. I've been all over doing it. I've been up to Durham University, Lilleshall and over to America; and to the grottiest little village hall, the back of beyond. But if you do it properly and tell people what you're trying to do, talk to parents about it, it can be of enormous significance for young people. It gives them stature; it gives them a big insight into themselves. You learn to work with others; you learn to play with and against people; you learn to conduct yourself properly – all those good things. That's why it's important. But this business of players projecting – the image thing... They can't be perfect all the time, because you can't be perfect all the time, but when they're in the public eye that's when I feel they should do their very best – Mr Beckham has shown everyone what is possible.

PD on the Beautiful Game

The game doesn't need racism or bad press, does it? Because football's become such a big thing. It's grown to such a monstrous size, become such an influence on so many people. It's frightening, absolutely frightening. And what you are when you're involved in the game, you are for that particular period of your life the keeper of the game. It's in your care and needs to be handed on in a better condition than when you started.

PD on the not so beautiful game

They do treat you badly in football. One thing you can be sure about is that they'll pee on most players at some stage and it will often be from a great height. But if you realise that early on, when it comes sooner or later it won't be such a shock, and hopefully you will have made some provision for afterwards.

PD on Modern Management

What do you say to fourteen millionaires sitting facing you on the dressing room bench? How do you tell them to play?

I think that now good managers have to be good man managers. I feel Ferguson's forte is the fact that he realises that if you can keep a group, a set of lads together that know one another and start to trust one another, you can get the collective, we're all in this together, spirit.... It's, if you like, marrying together the different pieces, the traits that players have got, the different skills that go into the complete jigsaw – you've got to have the strength and pace, and above all the intelligence. If you feel you've got a good side with good technical players but they are not intelligent and don't understand the game, you'll be ineffective. If you can only play in one way you'll be unsuccessful in the long run.

PD on Modern Football at the Highest Level

The biggest difference in football today is without doubt the pitches. The pitches at the top level are now wonderful to play on.... It's made the game quicker. The balls too are better... The players are much better and fitter, they spend a lot more time on technique, control is better – they're great ball manipulators. It makes them look better. It's more of an entertainment. It's great theatre. I watched Rivaldo under lights at the Nou Camp, so I am certain.

PD on the New Meadow

I've always wanted my ashes scattered in the centre-circle. When I wrote my last will I put a last line that if the Meadow is no longer there I'd like them thrown off the English Bridge so they'd be floating past the Meadow. I've asked for that. I think I'll have it done on a Saturday afternoon just after kick off at 3.00 p.m. I'm a bit of a romantic.

On the serious side, I realise that football's got to move on and small clubs have got to move on too.

The layperson's guide to football terminology – Number 1

"Early doors"

September Blues

"Even when you're dead, you must never allow yourself just to lie down and be buried." – Gordon Lee

What strikes me forcibly at times about this business of watching football is that, although I get older, the players I am watching never age. They are always mostly in their twenties, with occasional players not yet out of their teens or still fit enough and lucky enough to be running around in their early thirties. The team is an ever metamorphosing entity, that sloughs off the no longer wanted, the maimed, the disenchanted, the passenger, the unfulfilled potential. Just as it discards, so it is itself deserted by those with talent or ambition above the team's level or purse. For no two consecutive seasons is the playing-staff the same; it is even a rarity that the same team will turn out for consecutive games, and the composition of a team that starts a game is invariably tinkered with before the end. This constant flux and re-invention means that we watch more an illusion of a team than a team and it will always keep its youth. I meanwhile have gone from the pre-school boy listening at home to the litany of the weekly Saturday reading of the football results to a fifty-something contemplating what the experience of watching football will be like in my retirement. The eternal youth of the football-player allows the spectator to continue his football playing by proxy.

Football is essentially ephemeral. A run, a pass, a dummy, a cross, a shot, a goal – all happen in an instant, and, despite this being the age of the action replay, have immediately passed into another world. Whole games likewise slide into a past in which they merge with many other games, and may provide the odd memorable moment. Football is to do with the life and immediacy of the current game, but it is also greatly concerned with memories.

This ephemerality is linked to the fact that teams (and players and managers) are judged on their last result (or, more fairly perhaps, on their last performance). A team can win the Cup on Saturday and be relegated on Monday. There is no time for resting on laurels, and for this reason results have to be instant. How many football managers have the leisure to plan; to have a vision and be allowed the time to realise it? How many football managers expect to see the end of their contract? They sign up with great hope but know in their hearts that history is against them.

Mansfield Town 2 Salop 1
Luke Rodgers scores early on and Town eventually lose to a last minute goal. Oh well.

Town 4 Kidderminster Harriers 0
I had intended to be there, but work, the bane of the football spectator, came in the way. I was in school before 8 o'clock in the morning, but it was "open day" so I didn't leave until about 7.20 pm. Not only was I rather tired, but Small Heath to Shrewsbury in less than half an hour without any tea is not on. Not only did I miss what sounds like a stunning Town performance, but another Luke Rodgers hat-trick. How long is it since any Town player scored one hat-trick, let alone two within a few months. If we can hang onto him till the

end of the season, and he maintains this sort of form, we should be in with a realistic chance of promotion. Second in the table can't be bad for a start. Bring on Saturday and Rochdale; the memory of what Luke did to them at home last season should put them at a disadvantage before we start. Jagielka scored the other goal.

Saturday 22nd September, 2001

"An inch or two either side of the post and that would have been a goal." – Dave Bassett

Rochdale (home); Football League Division Three

Previous record in league games:					
Home			Away		
Win	Draw	Lose	Win	Draw	Lose
6	2	5	3	3	7

1-0 (HT 0-0); L.Rodgers (90)
Attendance: 4,612
Standpoint: For most of the game, on the Riverside, again leaning against a barrier just in front of the band; for the last five minutes, standing behind the goal at the Wakeman End.

This game was always going to be settled by just the one goal, but so nearly wasn't.

The crowds along the approach from the Column and in the Abbey Foregate area as I drove in were reminiscent of the old Division Two days. Expectation was obviously high after last Tuesday's performance and for a game involving the teams currently occupying the top two places in the division. Inside the ground it didn't seem so very crowded but it was still probably the highest gate I had known for a while. They were in good voice, the chants including the prophetic "We'll be number one at five o'clock". At one point someone also pointed out to the Rochdale fans that it is "Shrewsbury" not "Shrowsbury" (unless of course one has allegiance to Shrowsbry

School).

The composition of the team is now quite well established. The only change from a fortnight ago was that Karl Murray was back in, at the expense of Peter Wilding. This was probably only a matter of time. There is now genuine strength in depth, with the likes of Dunbavin, Lowe, Tretton and Wilding sitting on the bench. It is therefore up to those on the pitch to perform well enough to keep their places, which I think they probably did today. I was even impressed with Rioch's performance; he has not struck me as either a reliable defender or as offering width and support to attacks, but there were several good tackles and crosses today.

The first half was virtually all Salop, but there were chances at both ends. Salop's best chance was when Nigel Jemson headed over from the edge of the six yard box. The goalkeeper repeatedly spilled the ball when stopping shots, but no-one was following up. His kicking was erratic too, so he deserved the shouts of "Dodgy keeper". The contest was competitive but relatively clean. Neither trainer came on, which is remarkable these days.

The second half was more finely balanced, with Rochdale having more of the play than they had had before the break and being prepared to come forward. The game was already into extra time when Luke Rodgers took the ball past at least three defenders and scored a brilliant individual goal. So fleet-footed was he, they may as well have been wooden posts hammered into the ground. He immediately tore off his shirt and wheeled away only to be buried beneath a heap of team-mates. The shirt removal was obviously a reference to when he did the same after his hat-trick at Rochdale and was sent off for his over-enthusiasm. He knew that a change in the law meant he could repeat the gesture with impunity this time.

The referee was quite well in control throughout the game. He let a lot of petty things go and dismissed several dubious appeals. The bookings he gave seemed somewhat random, but at least he was consistent in his inconsistency.

My sugar today was emblazoned with the image of Charles Darwin, a thoroughly relevant icon in view of his links with Shrewsbury.

There are reports in *The Shropshire Star* that various clubs are interested in Luke. These include Sunderland who deny knowing anything about it and according to the report claim they would want better quality than Luke. This probably means that they will sign him within the month. He may be small, and he may be facing only Third Division defences, but how many players are capable of the goals he has created this season?

Before the game they were distributing leaflets with news of progress on the New Meadow. The leaflet started with a few points about the importance of the club to the town and what the New Meadow would offer to the people of Shrewsbury. It stated that the planning application had been submitted to the council and would be considered in the new year; that on Monday the full council would consider the recommendation of the cabinet that the council take over responsibility for the cost of the community facilities within the plan; and that, dependant on cost, the stadium design might fill in the corners to create a "bowl". The leaflet finished by urging fans to keep writing letters and maintaining the public debate over the issue (including explaining to "family and work colleges" [sic]). Fascinating stuff. What implications has it got for when a New Meadow might materialise, I wonder?

Open letter to the council (sent to *The Shropshire Star* via e-mail):

This may be yet another letter on the subject of the New Meadow. However, I write as a Salopian in exile, who nevertheless feels that I should have some say in a matter that is quite important to me. There is also a sense in which, because I am able to be more detached than residents of Shrewsbury, I can see the picture with less emotional colour.

During the 1980s Shrewsbury had a football team that was among the top forty five or so in the country. Many of the town's residents seemed unimpressed at the time by how remarkable this was. Since then the club's fortunes have waned until a couple of years ago it almost disappeared from the Football League. At that point some of the more indifferent citizens may have woken up to how important the club is to the town.

The team is currently thriving yet its supporters attend games in conditions that leave much to be desired, having improved little since the 1950s when the club first entered the League. One end of the ground is uncovered. The toilet facilities would not be out of place in the Third World. Catering facilities are limited. There is not so much as a scoreboard.

It is obviously a critical moment in the history of the club. If the town wishes to continue to appreciate the value of hearing on Saturday afternoon radio the likes of "Shrewsbury Town Two, Cheltenham Town One", then the council must get its act together and sort out the issues surrounding the New Meadow.

Tuesday 25th September

Salop are away to Swansea tonight and away again on Saturday. If they are still in the top three after that maybe we can start taking promotion seriously.

Salop featured in the "What Happened Next" section of *A Question of Sport* last night. It was Nigel Jemson's goal against Brighton last season, and it shows what a state I am in already after only a couple of weeks' teaching that I wasn't totally sure of the answer even though I was there. The answer of course was that a streaker appeared, and that was only a few weeks after a streaker at the away game at Kidderminster which I also witnessed. I don't know whether it was the same deluded gentleman.

Swansea 3 Salop 3

By all accounts not an inspiring performance, but who cares when you get an away point. Still second in the table, with 20 points from 10 games. What would the bookmakers have given for that before the season started? The scorers were Jemson (2; one a penalty) and Murray.

Wrexham have sacked Brian Flynn, their manager of umpteen

years. Inevitably, being Welsh, Kevin Ratcliffe is much mentioned. What are the odds firstly on him being offered the job and secondly on him taking it? In some ways the Shrewsbury fans have not truly taken him to their hearts even yet. There are some managers that the fans love. Arthur Rowley and Graham Turner are probably the best examples, and maybe it is connected to the fact that they were also players, but more than that players so obviously dedicated to the cause. This was of course also true for Jake King, but although he started with the fans' full backing he never achieved the success of Messrs Rowley and Turner and the love affair turned sour. Kevin Ratcliffe had a successful career at the top level, including captaining his country, but somehow he was not the unanimous choice of the people here. Perhaps it is to his credit that he has ignored the courting of popularity and channelled his energies into improving the performance and fortunes of the team. If he sticks with it, and Shrewsbury continue their revival, he may yet go down in history as one of our most loved and respected managers.

Scunthorpe United 3 Salop 1

So Salop are no longer in the top three, despite another Luke Rodgers goal. One point from two away games might have been welcome over the past few years, but somehow the expectation built up this season makes it disappointing. Still, there is another top of the table clash to look forward to at the Meadow next weekend – Friday night to be precise, as England play Greece on Saturday.

October 1st

"I see the world as a football, kicked about by the higher powers, with me clinging on by my teeth and toenails to the laces." – Dan Leno

I had the strangest dream last night. All right, most dreams are strange, but there were several oddities about this one. For one thing I rarely remember my dreams. Secondly this was about football, which is not a usual subject for my dreams when I do remember them (– perhaps this writing about the game is having an influence on my subconscious). I was spectator at a football match. It was not a stadium I recognised despite the fact that Shrewsbury Town were playing. That was weird enough, but the really odd thing was that each side consisted of just three players, a goalkeeper and two outfield players. One of the Town players was Steve Jagielka but I cannot say who the other players or the other team were, although I may have known as I was "watching". The game seemed to go on for a long time but there was only one goal (scored by the Town outfield player who was not Jagielka with a chip over the goalkeeper). I was there observing this game taking place, but I was also detached enough to think: "They can't carry a game on if there's only this number of players, can they?" "They ought to be getting really tired doing all this running around." Perhaps I should dream football more often, so long as Salop win.

I hear that Lennie the Lion, a.k.a. Ron Miller, was voted the best team mascot by his fellow mascots.

Footballers have always been the barometers of tonsorial taste, be it for brylcreamed locks, an unkempt Jesus-look, perm, shaven head, or whatever. Generally speaking a player's hairstyle dates his playing days as accurately as a tree's rings tell its age or carbon-dating reveals the secrets of even more ancient times. It is as accurate if not more so than the style of the strip or boots he wears.

Whether they lead fashion, follow it, or (having little else on their minds) are just amazingly in tune with it, it is difficult to say. With the exception of icons such as Kevin Keegan and David Beckham, I would suspect few are fashion leaders and even the most fashion conscious young man, such as David Ginola, does not necessarily have boys aping his hairstyle. Similarly, although arguably one of the greatest footballers of all time, there were certainly precious few modelling their locks in imitation of Bobby Charlton's distinctive "combed-over" style.

Friday 5th October, 2001

"It's now 1-1, an exact reversal of the score on Saturday." – Radio 5 Live

Hull City (home); Football League Division Three

Previous record in league games:					
Home			Away		
Win	Draw	Lose	Win	Draw	Lose
7	5	6	3	6	9

1-1 (HT 1-0); L.Rodgers (16)
Attendance: 5,010
Standpoint: On the Riverside, leaning against a barrier, twenty yards to the left of the half-way line. (N.B. a deliberate shift away from the band, which – good though they are – were a bit much on the eardrums from only a few yards distance.)

Evening games have their own unique flavour. The dark somehow makes for a more intimate atmosphere and despite the brilliance of the floodlights there always seems to be a sense that one's perception of the action is less certain. There is also the fact that the lights make visibility more difficult when the ball is kicked up in the air. You cannot easily see the ball against the lights and the zone above the pool of light cast by the floodlights appears disproportionately obscure. Perhaps that is part of the psychological reason for the increased cosiness. We become like cavemen huddling around the fire, hoping it will protect us from whatever lurks in the darkness beyond.

Tonight it is dark an hour or so before kick-off. There is cloud cover, with some light rain before the crowd is gathered in. It should be a good crowd with "big spending" Hull currently second in the table. Copies of *The Shropshire Star* (who incidentally printed my letter on Tuesday – with text unaltered but a few changes to paragraphing) were being distributed free outside the ground and made a lot of Hull's Faroese signing Julian Johnsson. I look forward to seeing him in the flesh, as obviously do the surprising number of Hull supporters who have made the long journey here.

A cracking game, Gromit. Two good teams going at each other positively for most of the game. The rain came on quite heavily in the second half, swirling in the beams of the floodlights like snowflakes. For ninety minutes Shrewsbury looked like worthy winners, but, as is the way with this game, we conceded an equaliser in injury time – a minute after Jemson's free-kick had hit the post. It wouldn't be fair to say that Shrewsbury suffered this time through sitting on a one goal lead. They did go for more, and could have had a hatful if all the chances had been taken. Still, it is probably significant that after Jagielka, who I thought had an excellent game, the other two players to catch the eye were the full-backs, Rioch and Moss. Incidentally, am I alone in thinking Jagielka a Bono (of U2) look-alike? Similarly Nigel Jemson bears more than a passing resemblance to the dashing Sergeant Troy – not the cad in *Far from the Madding Crowd*, but the young detective in the Midsomer Murders.

Hull City are called the Tigers, but in their kit they're not dissimilar to the Wolves. A suitable headline for a match report might be:

SHREWS MAUL TIGERS 1 – 1

Disappointing it may be to have to settle for one point, but you have to be philosophical and accept that in football there is often a twist. At least this year we had the goal first so a last minute goal did not leave us completely empty handed as it seems to have so often recently. Moreover as spectators we should be celebrating the standard of entertainment; as the bloke next to me remarked at half-time, "That was worth anyone's ten quid."

My sugar-sachet, which I am beginning to treat rather in the nature of a fortune cookie (or, probably more appropriately, like the jokes and riddles that drop out of crackers) informed me: "In 1936 the BBC began transmitting the first regular TV service in the world". Let no man say that football matches are not educational. Just hold in your mind for a moment the implications of that inoffensive seeming little sentence. Before that date there could be no Match of the Day nor any of the fifty soaps that now fill up the TV viewer's waking hours.

The Salop-Hull game was to prove much better entertainment than the England-Greece game the following day. This match was the reason that the Salop game and several others were played on Friday. Like the Salop game it was a draw, courtesy of an injury-time equaliser, but there the similarity ends. At least it means that England qualify for the World Cup, and football consequently gets a higher profile in the country, which in turn could translate into higher gates at the bread-and-butter games, such as the ones that feature Shrewsbury Town..

Blackburn Rovers have just beaten West Ham United 7-1. I remember when Salop scored seven against Blackburn. How footballing fortunes change; though maybe Salop fortunes are on the turn at the moment, particularly with results like....

Leyton Orient 2 Town 4

The "fan-scene" pages on Teletext are often amusing and give the somewhat differing, even bizarre, perspectives of fans of other clubs. This week a Leyton Orient page was bemoaning their fortune and the fact that manager Tommy Taylor had gone after suffering the humiliation of "losing to a fat pub side and Luke Rodgers". This was rather unkindly put I thought, but nicely balanced by a Southend fanzine page delighting in their neighbours' discomfort. The Southend page began: "One-nil down, then the opposition were crushed by excellent attacking football and the lads ran out 4-2 winners. But enough of Shrewsbury against Orient...."

For the record, the Town scorers were Rodgers (2), Jagielka and Redmile.

Town 0 Chesterfield 1

Saturday's winning display in London was followed up with defeat in the LDV Trophy by Chesterfield on Tuesday night (Chesterfield, a town where it's not just the church spire that's crooked apparently). They are in a higher division and, although not doing brilliantly, a couple of seasons ago would have torn Salop apart. I would have gone but was too tired for the stage of term and needing to be alert on

Wednesday. Apparently Salop were unlucky to lose, with the rare spectacle of a missed Jemson penalty and the not so rare winning goal in injury time. No one should leave a Salop game before the final whistle if they want to see all the goals. We can console ourselves that it was only a nothing competition and that the league is more important. That is only true to an extent; winning is always important, it is a good habit to acquire, it breeds confidence, and winning any competition would be nice. Darlington this coming Saturday means another near the top of the table clash.

All-time Salop Favourites Number Three – Alf

"Strangely, in slow motion replay, the ball seemed to hang in the air for even longer." — David Acfield

Alf Wood seemed as solid as if he had been hewn from the rock in the Dingle in Shrewsbury's Quarry. He was uncompromising, unflinching, tough, yet deceptively athletic. – One of my abiding memories of him is of a goal he scored by seemingly hanging in the air an inordinate length of time and twisting to head in a ball that had come back off the bar. He was a rarity in being equally effective in attack or defence. Forwards did not mess with Alf when he was centre-half and defenders were brushed aside when he led the attack. A line from one of the contemporary terrace songs went: "Oh Alfie Wood – is wonderful / Oh Alfie Wood is wonderful" (to a tune vaguely resembling *When The Saints Go Marching In*). It must, however, be conceded that much of his effectiveness relied on instilling terror into the opposition and cultivating a reputation that preceded him and did a lot of his work for him.

Alf Wood was born in Macclesfield on 25th October 1945 and began his career with Manchester City, for whom he signed in June 1963. He had been an England Youth International but this early promise appeared to have come to nothing when he failed to make the grade at City, being sold onto Salop after making only 24 appearances in three years.

He was with us for six years, making 257 League appearances (plus one as sub), 15 in the F.A. Cup and 11 in the League Cup. It was at

Salop that he was converted from centre-half to striker, which conversion was so successful that in the 1971-2 season he scored 40 League and cup goals (including FIVE in the home game against Blackburn, Nina). On the strength of this he was sold by the Club to Millwall who paid what was for them a club record of £44,000. His sale proved one of the final straws for Harry Gregg who resigned as manager a few months afterwards. Altogether Alf scored 65 League goals for Salop, and a further 4 in the F.A. Cup and 5 in the League Cup. Many of these goals came from the penalty spot. Let's face it, no sane goalkeeper would have got in the way of a shot from Alf Wood delivered from a mere 11 metres.

Alf was with Millwall from June 1972 until he signed for Hull City in November 1974. He scored 38 goals for Millwall in 99 League games. His portrayal in Eamon Dunphy account of the first of those seasons is illuminating. Not only is the strength of Alf's personality apparent (he is soon the king of the dressing-room) but there is some reference to a parsimonious streak that goes to the extent of charging others for the cups of tea he has bought. At Hull he scored 10 goals in 51 League games before moving to Middlesbrough in October 1976. Here his tally was a modest 2 goals in 22 games and at the end of the season he went to Walsall where he managed only 2 in 26 games. After that he was in non-league football with Stafford Rangers – but at least he got a trip to Wembley (and scored) when they won the F.A. Trophy in 1979.

Saturday 20th October, 2001

"Five days shalt thou labour, as the Bible says. The seventh day is the Lord thy God's. The sixth day is for football...." – Anthony Burgess

Darlington (home); Football League Division Three

Previous record in league games:					
Home			Away		
Win	Draw	Lose	Win	Draw	Lose
6	2	3	3	3	5

Attendance: 0
Standpoint: By the gate on the avenue to the Gay Meadow.

good start to the day overflow from loft fixed easier than anticipated just replace ballcock amazingly heavy like sponge absorbing water no buoyancy left fell off with merest touch hadnt been in loft for some time such a bind putting up the steps and climbing into dust and cobwebs never too convinced theres not mice just a matter of emptying some water out so i could screw on plastic ballcock we had from some earlier plumbing adventure i was glad of a sit down and cup of coffee after that we drove straight to salop to check out glasses for pen she got them here before even found in coleham replacement spare ballcock and another arm to fix bathroom flushing mechanism no rain after we left home but considerable standing water on some roads tasty veggie dinner shopping for jacket and trousers for me amazingly easy first shop we came to had suitable jacket in window wouldnt be that simple in birmingham bloke in shop had worked in tailors on new street said people came here from all over the country customer said he was off to watch ireland versus england rugby on tv why not watch shrewsbury town live i thought time for a couple of other shops before i left pen in powneys told her to look for mcewans atonement wyle cop seems fairly quiet no sign of wrekin today with mist shutting out distance looks as if mansers art shop is still open how many of their different lines will move into the new premises being built beside gyratory how many times have i walked over this bridge the water seems high and brown but still some way below path plenty of birdlife not much noise from the ground dodging dawdling shoppers english bridge rebuilt in 1925 etcetera im slightly early no sign of police no stewards directing traffic no programme sellers no great press no golden goal ticket sellers cars parked along approach to ground in large red letters on white board fastened to gate MATCH OFF others equally taken aback is the pitch waterlogged ive just looked said one i reckon they made the decision too early the pitch seems fine i never dreamed the game would be off it never entered my head have we really had that much rain they said nothing on the radio but we havent had the radio on since eight oclock

I wrote earlier that communication has greatly improved and perhaps implied that it was unlikely that I should again turn up for a match that had been called off. John, my brother-in-law, did try to phone me to tell me this match was off, but we had already left home by then. Oh well.

Tuesday 23rd October, 2001

"In terms of the Richter Scale this defeat was a force eight gale." – John Lyall

Rushden and Diamonds (home); Football League Division Three

Previous record in league games:					
Home			Away		
Win	Draw	Lose	Win	Draw	Lose
–	–	–	–	–	–

0-2 (HT 0-1)
Attendance: 4016
Standpoint: On the Riverside, leaning against a barrier just a shade towards the half-way line from the band's area. (They were missing again tonight. Were their instruments still waterlogged from Saturday or did they know something?)

Tonight is the first time Salop have played Rushden and Diamonds in a League game. They did meet in the F.A. Cup a couple of years ago, but we won't mention that – as someone said on the way into the ground: "We owe these Diamonds one.". Although manager Brian Talbot is relatively famous from his days with Ipswich and Arsenal, the Rushden team is largely unknown to me. They do come here on a seven game unbeaten streak and the gist of Kevin Ratcliffe's message on Radio Shropshire tonight is: "Don't underestimate Rushden and Diamonds". Did you tell your team that, Kevin?

The Salop team is becoming quite settled, several players being ever-present or virtually so. I hope that "settled" does not mean stale or complacent. One exception to the status quo is that Ian Dunbavin gets another chance in goal tonight. Ryan Lowe will be on the right side. On the injury front Jamie Tolley is getting fitter; this should be a good thing in terms of competition for places.

It is appreciably darker than the equivalent time for the Hull game a couple of weeks ago. The pitch is resplendently green after its recent watering. The scene is set for a spectacle of fine football....

Let's be honest, the better team on the night won. Bill Turley was probably the most solid looking keeper I've seen this year. They had several tall competitive defenders. They worked together well as a team and looked dangerous at times when going forward. In contrast Salop were sadly below par, like someone with flu before they've recognised the symptoms, a watch whose battery is starting to run down, an engine with sand in the oil, a sonnet whose lines refuse to rhyme, a symphony plagued by dissonances and discords, a party of strangers playing blind-man's-buff. The game was a (timely?) sobering reminder of what it really means to be a Shrewsbury Town supporter – that there will always be games like this, where there is practically nothing to cheer for ninety minutes; where it all descends to the level of a pantomime of misdirected passes, mistimed tackles, weak shots and uncoordinated thinking; where the football brains have switched off, natural instinct goes AWOL along with good habits learned from a lifetime's experience, and the only tactic is to hit high balls from the back.

There was one brief (I first typed "grief": Freudian slip?) – one brief early passage of beautifully flowing interpassing which ended with Jags missing the target, but the true tone of Salop's play for the evening was set by the most inept corner-kick it has been my misfortune to witness. Greg Rioch fluffed his kick and succeeded only in giving away a free kick by the corner flag. Is it asking too much of a professional footballer that he can kick a stationary football when no opposition player is allowed near him? The other incident that summed up Town's evening was when a potentially important attacking pass was magnificently intercepted by the referee and

Rushden were set away again.

Scarcely able to believe how poor Salop were, Rushden scored two. The first crept inside Dunbavin's right-hand post, the second had more of a suspicion of offside, but then we were in the hands of an assistant referee with a very individual understanding of the offside law. At one point Luke Rodgers received the ball in a position two or three yards offside but was not flagged despite being right under the assistant referee's nose. Maybe the gentleman was looking over Luke's head and hadn't even noticed him.

The pitch may have been no longer waterlogged, but too many of the Salop team conducted themselves as if they believed they were wading through mud. Significantly Nigel Jemson had reverted to the whinging moaner of last year, no longer urging and encouraging others, no longer the trusty and mature fulcrum of the team. Mark Atkins was statuesque. Karl Murray was ineffectual. Ryan Lowe (who did hit the metalwork with a well-taken free-kick) and Steve Jagielka ran round in circles, became infected with the general desire to kick the ball to the opposition, and were substituted. The most positive thing to say about Luke Rodgers's performance is that I hope there were lots of scouts watching. If there were, they may not return, and he might still be with us come Christmas. To be fair to Luke, he received little in the way of decent service; he cannot be expected to outjump someone eighteen inches taller; he needs the ball at his feet. The most impressive Town players were Mick Heathcote and Matt Redmile, but you don't want your central defenders to be the ones that catch the eye – and they were two of the worst offenders in terms of launching high balls forward. The management were equally inept; they replaced Jagielka, who bustles about and occasionally looks dangerous in the opposition area, with Iain Jenkins, who sat in the middle of the defence at a time when we needed to be attacking. Let's hope the patient recovers by the next game....

This was the sort of performance which is supposed to send supporters home in a mood to beat the wife or kick the cat. Me, I'm much too fatalistic for that. It is after all only a game. Beside, by the time I get home my wife will be asleep, blissfully unaware of the torments I have been suffering, and we don't have a cat. Still, at least the trip was made worthwhile by the sight of the Abbey, which was truly majestic, lit up against the night sky.

One other consolation is that when the fare on the pitch is less than inspiring one is often more aware of the comments made by the crowd. These are largely a combination of the banal, negative and unrepeatable, but one or two can bring a smile on a dark evening. Two I remember from tonight were: "Kick it, you [expleted deleted] ballet dancer!" (to the Rushden goalkeeper) and "This referee would make a good bus-driver."

At half-time, former Meadow favourite (a euphemism for "the crowd didn't moan at him excessively"), Carleton Leonard (Salop, 1975-83) was on the pitch. He also features in the matchday programme, and, although he looks cheerful and well, the picture of a bespectacled skinhead is a little different from my memory of his long curly locks. It happens to us all, Carleton.

Today's sugar-sachet: "Horatio Nelson 1758-1805 [that's a very high-scoring game] – Defeated the French fleet at Trafalgar in 1805". Perhaps in the next World Cup we would fare better if we challenged the French to play on water again.

The layperson's guide to football terminology – Number 2

"The goalkeeper made himself big."

24th October

"He's one of those footballers whose brains are in his head." – Derek Johnstone (BBC TV Scotland)

Salop were on *A Question of Sport* again tonight. The picture board featured a shot of Lennie the Lion sitting in a coracle on the flooded Meadow pitch. They guessed it was Shrewsbury Town, although John Parrott (Snooker-player, TV personality and Everton fan) didn't know the name of the ground. They didn't know Lennie's name, not even being too clear what sort of animal he is. Mind you, Ally McCoist (Scottish International footballer, TV personality and cheeky chappy) didn't know the name of Kilmarnock's squirrel either (Kilmarnock being his club at that time). We seem to get more than our fair share of publicity on such programmes.

The other thing I spotted on TV was in the Oxford United "fan-scene" Teletext page. It seems that our old friend Mr Redcard upset them on Saturday. I checked the statistics: he sent off two Oxford players towards the end of the game. They obviously feel as aggrieved as we did over the Hartlepool game. How much longer will he be allowed to roam through the Third Division creating havoc in his wake? Will his effect be spread around evenly or will he make the crucial difference as to which sides are promoted or relegated? — The after-effects of this did indeed spread further. The Oxford manager, Mark Wright (former England defender), would be given a four-match touchline ban and also suspended by the club for alleged racial abuse of Mr Redcard. Racial abuse, if proven, is inexcusable, but I'm sure that the prime cause of this situation was the incompetence of the official, not the colour of his skin. Ian Atkins, former Meadow hero (1975-82) and manager of clubs too numerous to list, would be appointed director of football at Oxford during Wright's suspension (and beyond).

Torquay United 2 Town 1 (Rioch)

28th October

"Foote balle, wherein is nothinge but beastlie furie and exstreme violence." – Sir Thomas Elyot (1490-1546)

This week there was an episode of *The Simpsons* that featured what the Americans refer to as "soccer". Association Football is a minority sport in the States. It is regarded as mainly something for girls to play (which they actually do very well, having one of the top women's teams in the world). There are, however, many Americans for whom football is a mystery second only to cricket. When I introduced my friend Dale to its arcane practices by taking him to see Salop playing at Reading in 1977 (we won 1-0), he was, I believe, genuinely amazed at how men could control a ball so well without resorting to using their hands. He was later to be disabused of any idea that Third Division English football represented any particularly high level of skill in this regard when he watched the World Cup on television and saw the likes of Brazil in action.

Anyway, to return to *The Simpsons*, the programme started with everyone going to watch a game of soccer. Unfortunately they considered it boring and a fight broke out that escalated into a fully blown riot. This encapsulated two points about the American view of soccer. Firstly it is boring because nothing much apparently happens and scoring is either low or non-existent. Secondly loutish behaviour and crowd violence are closely connected to it. Mat Groening and co. were no doubt being a little mischievous here, but there is often truth in jest. One needs to appreciate football's finer points to understand that a nil-nil draw can actually be engaging, enthralling, exciting, energising, cathartic, and so on; and just as the English might dismiss baseball as simply men playing rounders with big bats and ridiculous outfits, so Americans are entitled to mock soccer's little foibles.

The link between football and ill-mannered, antisocial, aggressive, yobbish behaviour is justified too, as I was reminded yesterday. We were travelling on a train from Manchester to Birmingham when a group of twenty or so Bristol City fans boarded the train at Stoke. They had obviously already been having a run-in with the local police who were massed on the platform and were no doubt relieved to get these oafs out of their hair. The police might have had some regard for the ordinary travelling public and accompanied them a little further, but they didn't. These young gentleman proceeded to march intimidatingly through the train in the direction of the buffet, chanting at the top of their voices and subjecting everyone to their views on Stoke City, Manchester United and the world generally. These views were expressed in language liberally laced with the sort of obscenities that should not be foisted upon the world at large, containing as it did small children and adults who might not wish to hear such words.

There was still plenty of noise and a generally menacing air, but they mostly stayed in the buffet until, as we neared Stafford, a few of them walked back very quietly through the train. At Stafford the train, which was already some three-quarters of an hour late getting down from Glasgow, seemed in no rush to depart and eventually a posse of police appeared. At that point we were informed over the intercom that we were delayed because of an incident on the train. The lads had obviously done something bad enough to warrant the police being sent for.

We had had enough of sitting there and decided to switch trains for another going on to Birmingham. It was obvious that one or two of the gentleman the police should have been interviewing had done the same, as we heard one making a comment that suggested that he had got the keys to the buffet. Our original train was approximately an hour and a half late arriving in Birmingham. What the police had achieved I do not know – very little, I suspect. However, what exercises my mind is that these immature and thoughtless morons, supported by alcohol and the strength of the mob, should so impinge on other people's right to peace and time. Whether their connection to football is crucial I am still not convinced, but football does unfortunately provide an excuse for them to gather together.

All-time Salop Favourites Number Four – Daisy

"He's very fast and if he gets a yard ahead of himself nobody will catch him." – Bobby Robson

Dave Roberts was born in Birmingham in December 1946. It may not be a universally held view, but he was, I believe, on his day the most exciting and possibly the most gifted winger we have had. Physically perhaps he was not in the Stanley Matthews-Diego Maradona mould of dribblers with a low-centre of gravity. Sometimes, however, he had a similarly demoralising effect on full-backs. Speed was not his greatest asset; indeed his progress down the wing often seemed languid. His ball-control, though adequate, never seemed brilliant and he moved in a gangling, jerky way. Nevertheless, he had the priceless gift of being able to send a left-back the wrong way. In his prime he could pass an unfortunate opponent at will and drop the ball into the box for the head of Alf Wood or George Andrews.

He didn't score many goals, but one stands out in the memory. For the home match against Aston Villa in the first of their two wilderness years in the Third Division, Dave Roberts was not only captain but scored the winner with as sweetly a struck shot as you will come across. This must have been delicious to Dave Roberts as Villa were the club who had given up on him after allowing him only a handful of opportunities whilst he was on their books. He had joined Villa as an apprentice, signing for them in December 1963. Villa was his local club – he had gone to school at Marsh Hill, a fraction over a mile from Villa Park. He played a mere fifteen games for them before joining Salop in March 1968. He was with us for six years, scoring 20 goals in 224 league appearances (plus 6 as sub) and one other goal in some 21 games in cup competitions. After leaving us he spent a season at Swansea City scoring once in 32 outings (plus 5 as sub).

His main shortcoming was that at times he seemed disinterested – let's face it, who would remain permanently interested in being the target of assorted Neanderthals whose only thought was to take your legs off at the knees? This less than hundred per cent commitment was not always popular with the crowd, nor was it universally admired by his fellow players, one of whom on one occasion gave him such a rollicking at half-time that the sensitive Mr Roberts did not manage to reappear after the interval. Many years ago I worked with one of his former school PE teachers who described him as laid-back. Mike

Fenton, another teaching colleague and friend, is a fellow old boy of his alma mater and recalls how Dave Roberts's sporting success was held up as an example to younger pupils.

Transatlantic View

"Nicky Butt – he's another aptly named player. He joins things, brings one sentence to an end and starts another." – Barry Davies

Following my reference above to *The Simpsons*, my mind was exercised concerning the mystery that football holds for so many in the world. I sent a slimmed-down copy of the first part of this book to Dale Kramer, inviting his comments. Dale responded:

"I very much enjoyed reading your soccer article. You got exactly right my impression back in 1977, saying I was amazed at how the ball could be controlled so intricately by the feet. I don't think a paragraph or two or three (indeed even an entire essay) could convey more than that one phrase does about the degree of my comprehension of soccer. I actually played a few Sunday morning 'games' of soccer (in an over-40 [years old] league) a few years ago, and from that experience I learned, from a negative angle, what excellent physical condition soccer players need to be in. I remember only two other distinct things from that playing experience: (1) I cleverly thought that by underkicking the ball I could sail it over the heads of the defenders and thus by outrunning the defenders could dash past them and resume control of the ball (it did work once or twice) and (2) in my eagerness not to be a totally incompetent player I evidently got a little physical and two different people complained (in the last game I played – no cause-and-effect connection, though) that I 'played rough'.

"As to your article, I agree with you that a good bit of prior knowledge is assumed, if not about soccer rules then about the names of teams in England and the different tiers of leagues/teams. This is not a negative comment, since with my fairly minimal knowledge of the subject I could follow nearly all of your commentary. But if your audience is going to be Americans who have never read British newspapers or attended any sort of soccer game, they may have a hard go.

"But it'd be worth it for them! Your style is very effective, in joshing about the quality of teams, jibing at referees' competence (being at Level 3 is no excuse), and referring to strategies of scoring. "Thanks for letting me read your article. Great fun!"

This shows several things, apart from what a generous and kind-hearted friend Dale is (even quietly putting me right about the date of the Reading game – I had originally written "1976"). It testifies how someone not brought up to the culture of association football can acquire an interest, although the starting point may have been a not particularly high quality game. Dale's remarks about his own experience of active involvement are illuminating, particularly the insight into fitness and how robust play often compensates for skill. His chip and run tactic sounds spectacular. It reminds me of what seems to happen all the time in rugby. I can't see it being generally effective in professional soccer, demanding as it does both terrific accuracy and speed, although I can think of examples, such as Gazza's sublime goal against Scotland.

Saturday 3rd November, 2001
"The lads really ran their socks into the ground." – Sir Alex Ferguson

Lincoln City (home); Football League Division Three

Previous record in league games:					
Home			Away		
Win	Draw	Lose	Win	Draw	Lose
4	1	6	6	2	3

1-1 (HT 1-1); M.Heathcote (10)
Attendance: 3,437

Standpoint: Against a barrier in front of where the band are supposed to be (no signs of them again), immediately behind a pillar that I needed to dodge either side of to get a decent view.

That's another referee off Kevin Ratcliffe's Christmas card list. This one was not so dire for much of the game, but he had (magnificently abetted by an equally incompetent assistant referee) a nightmare half minute which effectively deprived Town of two points. In that half minute the two officials overlooked a handball by a Lincoln player, ignored an obvious offside and gazed with admiration as the player, Dave Cameron, bore down on Mark Cartwright. The inevitable following link in this chain of events was that Cartwright brought Cameron down on the edge of the box. From where I was standing (level with the incident) this appeared to be just outside the box. What happened next was that the two officials were forced by their own ineptitude to send off Cartwright, as he was the last defender. They compounded their ineptitude and the amount they were penalising Salop by also deciding that it should be a penalty.

Up until that moment things had gone quite well. Mark Cartwright had replaced Ian Dunbavin (though not for long, as it turned out). Leon Drysdale was back in the team at right back and Darren Moss was pushed up into midfield instead of Ryan Lowe. After a nervous few minutes at the beginning the format seemed to be working and Town deserved the lead which came from a rocket off the foot of Mick Heathcote. There was further Town pressure, including a Jagielka shot hitting the bar, a couple of corners, a free-kick and Moss heading over the bar. It was very much against the run of play that Lincoln got their equaliser from Holmes's penalty kick.

Thereafter Lincoln were completely lacking in adventure. The only side to make the running was ten-man Town. It was heartening to see the way the team as a unit and as individuals kept working away. We never looked under any pressure and were unlucky not to gain better reward. I do not begrudge the points that Rushden took away from the Meadow because they played for them; but it is galling that teams turning in performances so uninspired and of such wretched calibre as offered by Hartlepool and Lincoln should pilfer points merely because of the fallibility of officials. Statistically there should be comfort in the cliché that over the season matters will even out....

In contrast to the way Town's efforts to rise above poor opposition were frustrated, the Gay Meadow witnessed this afternoon two instances of successful and dramatic flight. At the beginning of the first half a hot-air balloon came over. It was advertising a certain petrol, which I won't name (although it is what I put in my own car). It drifted slowly and serenely away to flirt with the low lying clouds. Near the start of the second half we were treated to the sight of two swans flying over. They truly are impressive, a combination of power and beauty. The down-beat of their wings makes a unique and instantly recognisable sound as they speed straight and sure as pure white darts.

Crowd witticism of the day (to a player taking a long time to complete a throw-in) was: "You'll be as bald as I am by the time you take this!" This was not uttered by me, though I can empathise with the man's consciousness of his own shiny-headedness as well as admire his readiness to offer it in the cause of humour.

My sugar sachet proclaims "Man on the Moon, 20 July 1969". So, it is over thirty years since we put a man on the moon, but we still can't find decent referees to officiate at Third Division football games.

It is worth remarking on the topsy-turvy nature of the results between these two clubs. The results are well balanced but historically both teams have done better away from home, which is certainly a rarity in Town's case.

The rumour factory has taken on a complete extra shift once again. The latest off the production line are that Spurs want Luke Rodgers for £1.75 million and that Stockport County want Kevin Ratcliffe. The latter's reaction is that such interest – in him and in the players – is a healthy sign, as it means that the Club must be doing well if others covet the staff. He certainly comes across as a sensible man; the more I hear him the more I am confirmed in this opinion – his comments on matches are usually spot on.

Poetic Interlude Two – *Homer's Tale*

"We're football people, not poets, but obviously I'm disappointed with the result." –Mick McCarthy

As is the rule in civilised warfare,
The matrons and the maids remain behind;
So, dearest my Penelope, did you,
Whilst I, the modern Odysseus, fully armed
With packed lunch and umbrella, went to join
The current form of battle, called football.

A long journey I had, by courtesy
Of British Rail, in trains just faster I
Am told than Attic ships, and possibly
More water-tight. I sailed by the canal
As far as Wolverhampton; disembarked
To mingle with a host of gallant troops
Athirst to ransack Troy. – Bold warriors
They (veritable Wolves), the nation's youth
Let loose by parents' fond neglect to run
Its Saturday riot of grown-up ways:
Boys buying beers in railway buffet-rooms,
And smoking, swearing, shouting, just like dad.
Another train eventually arrived,
And sometime later left. The sea was smooth,
But soon the Wrekin-wave reared up on high,
And others rolled along the Welsh horizon.
We passed through country of my youth, and came
At last near to the ancient Battlefield
Of Shrewsbury Town.

Of journey I sing here –
Elsewhere of wars. (May it suffice to say
They don't make wooden horses as they did.)
The weary battle ended, I pack up;
My monthly pilgrimage to Shrewsbury

Complete. Now tired as Odysseus after
The war, the exercise of wit, and all
The wandering, I too return homeward.
The journey back, although at night, sadly
Lacks all the excitement of his. Also
The whistle went and he had won; not I.
Add too the pains of being my own Homer.
— The consolation that I own is this:
That you will greet me with a wifely kiss,
And, having worked at crochet not the loom,
Will welcome gladly home your errant groom.

Written circa 1976, when I was newly married and didn't drive so much as a milk-float. It is sad that I should even consider it necessary now to point out that "Homer" has nothing to do with The Simpsons.

Tuesday 6th November, 2001

"I'm not a believer in luck..... but I do believe you need it." – Alan Ball

Darlington (home); Football League Division Three
3-0 (HT 0-0); D.Moss (71), N.Jemson (pen., 74), L.Rodgers (79)
Attendance: 3084
Standpoint: Against a barrier twenty yards to the right of where I was on Saturday.

For most of the first half the only fireworks were those fountaining every now and then against the night sky. The referee almost lit the blue paper on a potentially volatile game; but somehow, although he had virtually lost control through his handling of the proceedings, matters calmed down. Some of his decisions were bizarre, such as awarding free-kicks against the player who was pushed or who had an opponent holding them down. Eventually, however, he realised how much of the dirt and negativity were coming from Darlington (as is witnessed by his final tally of five yellows and one red for Darlington against one questionable yellow for Salop).

The biggest cheer of the night was actually for Steven Gerrard. The Liverpool and England player had come to watch his mate Ian Dunbavin play and was persuaded to do the half-time draw. He did so to a chorus of "Gerrard is a Shrewsbury fan". Up to that point Mr Gerrard wouldn't have been too impressed, although his friend had accomplished a creditable double-save.

The game was transformed during the course of nine minutes. Darren Moss shot through a crowded goalmouth for a stunning goal. This seemed to take the tension out of Salop's play and within a couple of minutes we were 2 – 0 up, courtesy of a Jemson penalty after Luke Rodgers had been upended. Ultimately it was Darlington's failure to cope with Rodgers that undid them. Their only strategy for stopping him when he was through on a run was to scythe him down with all the subtlety of the Grim Reaper. This led to the penalty and several of the bookings. In addition, on one of the few occasions that their tactic failed, he skipped through to walk in his first goal in five outings. He might have been awarded another penalty in the last five minutes, but only gained a painful limp which caused his substitution. It is to be hoped this will not prove too serious.

The Darlington team has few star names but does include David Brightwell, one of the footballing sons of Olympic athletes Robbie Brightwell and Anne Packer. Robbie Brightwell is of course one of Shrewsbury's famous sons, whilst his wife won an Olympic gold in 1964 with an amazing run. I read an article recently about the likelihood of the children of great athletes inheriting the right genes to be world-class themselves. This was in the light of the imminent arrival of a son for Steffi Graf and André Agassi. What are the chances that he will be a Wimbledon champion? The Brightwell boys were given as limited evidence of instances where something appears to get passed on. I think.

My half-time sugar, informative as ever, tells me that James Watson and Francis Crick discovered the structure of DNA in 1953. This must have been round about the same time that I first glimpsed Shrewsbury Town in action, though I doubt there is any connection.

In interviews Kevin Ratcliffe emphasises the importance of the crowd. It could well be the same for all clubs as far as I know, but

Shrewsbury crowds although in many ways long-suffering tend to become impatient rather rapidly. They are often intolerant with what they perceive as poor refereeing. There are elements who single out individual players for criticism; there was apparently one fan who had a disagreement with Nigel Jemson at a recent game (a motif sadly to recur). The crowds at Shrewsbury also decline perceptibly following disappointing results. Thus, if you were to plot a graph showing the home attendances for this season so far, they rise steadily from 2,783 for Hartlepool United to a peak of 5,010 for Hull City, and thereafter mirror the falling away of point collection by the team.

The latest club reported to be showing interest in Luke Rodgers is West Bromwich Albion. Their manager, Gary Megson (who incidentally played two games for Salop back in September 1995), admits that they have been watching Luke. Following the collapse of their attempts to sign Danny Dichio from Sunderland (which are reported to have faltered for several reasons, including the size of his salary demands), Luke Rodgers would be an attractive proposition, coming from a lower division rather than from a Premiership squad. What Luke thinks of all this I do not know. I suspect, however, that his current slight dip in form might not be unconnected.

From the point of view of clubs like West Brom you can see the attraction of strengthening their squads by sweeping up any player from a lower division who shows any sign of rising above that level. From the points of view of Shrewsbury Town and Luke Rodgers matters are probably far more complex. For Salop there is a tension between holding onto talent that will improve their standing in the league and the financial realities which will always urge that they capitalise on any of that talent for which more affluent clubs are prepared to give money. As far as Luke is concerned, he has the problem not only of keeping his feet on the ground, but also of considering his career in the long term. Is it better to be the proverbial shark in the trout hatchery than to have to be avoiding on a weekly basis the unwanted attentions of thugs who have earned International caps for their ability to kick lumps out of centre forwards? Does it make sense to stay for the moment where you are successful, appreciated and have a seasoned pro like Nigel Jemson from whom to learn more about the trade? Or is the lure of playing for a club in a higher division too difficult to resist? Although of course there are glorious exceptions (such as Jim Holton, Nigel Pearson and Steve Ogrizovic), not many Town players have made a success of an upwards move. Carl Griffiths, Salop's previous goal-scoring teenager, for example, made little impact with Manchester City and has drifted through a long line of clubs back down to the Third Division.

Time alone will tell whether any of the speculation surrounding Luke amounts to anything more than just that. Whatever the outcome, I hope it is in the best interests of both Luke and Salop and that his performance on the pitch in the meantime is not unduly affected.

All-time Salop Favourites Number Five – Graham Turner

"What I said to them at half time would be unprintable on the radio." – Gerry Francis

If you want an indefatigable, whole-hearted rock of a centre-half or defensive mid-fielder, look no further than **Graham Turner**. Graham Turner came to Salop as an apparent journeyman defender and left as a legend. In the meantime he had made over four hundred appearances for Town (in all competitions), often as an inspirational, lead-by-example captain, but perhaps more importantly as arguably the most successful in a Salop's dynasty of successful player-managers. His predecessors, Rowley and Durban, both won promotion for the Town, but Graham Turner is the only Town manager to lead the club to the vertiginous heights of the old Second Division. He qualifies for inclusion in the list of my all-time greats not only as a player but also as my favourite manager. Indeed, my brother argues with a great deal of justification that winning the Third Division title (ahead of the wealth of Watford and Swansea), the Shropshire Senior Cup and the Welsh Cup in a year was a more difficult task to achieve than any treble won by managers of Liverpool or Manchester United.

Graham Turner was born in Ellesmere Port in October 1947. Like

Alf Wood he was an England Youth International. He started his professional career at Wrexham, signing for them in July 1965, and playing 77 League games in two and a half years. At the beginning of 1968 he moved to Chester City, where he stayed for five years. Here he scored five times in 215 League appearances (plus 3 as sub). Historically speaking that was nothing in comparison to his time at Salop. He signed for us on 1st January 1973 (as a replacement for Jim Holton who had signed for Manchester United) for what was at the time a Club record fee of £30,000. He scored 22 goals in 342 League appearances for us (plus 13 as sub), one goal in 27 F.A. Cup games, two goals in 17 League Cup games and three goals in 32 Welsh Cup games.

Graham Turner's time at Salop was arguably the period of the Club's greatest development. We had suffered relegation to the Fourth Division at the end of his first full season as a player, but after that matters improved. We bounced back immediately the following season. There were three years of consolidation in Division Three and then promotion as Champions in Turner's first year in charge. We spent a few seasons finding our feet in the Second Division but by the time Graham Turner departed we were comfortably in the top half of the table. His final game playing for Salop was in the team that drew with Wrexham in the second leg of the Final of the Welsh Cup in May 1984, thereby winning the Cup on aggregate score. At the end of that season he left us and thereafter became a full-time manager.

His managerial career has had its ups and downs, as is true of all football managers. He was Town's manager from November 1978 to July 1984; of the 243 games of his reign Salop won 86 and drew 73. He moved on in July 1984 to manage Aston Villa for what was possibly his least successful period. In two years his team lost 33 and drew 29 out of 105 games. He replied personally (and very nicely) when I wrote to him whilst he was there and sent two tickets to watch Villa. After he parted company with Deadly Doug he was picked up by Wolverhampton Wanderers. He had a great deal of success with Wolves, lifting them from Fourth to Second Division. His team won 164 and drew 102 out of 383 games. He was with Wolves some seven and a half years before becoming one in a line of managers who proved as disposable as Sir Jack Hayward's income. Since August 1995 he has been with Hereford, with a number of titles offering variations on Manager, Chairman and Director of Football. Apart from the disaster of Hereford being tipped out of the League by Brighton, his record there has been similar to his time at Shrewsbury.

A Brief Reply
"These managers all know their onions and cut their cloth accordingly." – Mark Lawrenson

"In reply to your letter concerning my inclusion in your book. The account is accurate and I must say very complimentary. Good luck with the project. I shall watch with interest for the day it becomes a best seller."

The layperson's guide to football terminology – Number 3

"Selling a dummy"

16th November, 2001
"And I suppose they [Spurs] are nearer to being out of the FA Cup now than at any other time since the first half of this season, when

they weren't ever in it anyway." –John Motson

It's Cup day tomorrow. Gone are the heady days when Salop didn't have to enter the first round. There's no other representative from Shropshire this year either. The trip to Brighton is a long one (particularly when followed up by travelling to Carlisle on Tuesday). After almost heading for the great football scrap-heap a few years back (sounds familiar?), Brighton are riding high in the Second Division and even Lee Steele is beginning to get mentioned. I admit I found him a disappointment when he was at Salop; he had undoubted ability, but the commitment often seemed less than wholehearted. My only trip to the now defunct Goldstone Ground (so long ago that it was before Brighton's rise to the top Division and the Cup Final) culminated in a bad defeat for Salop. Let's hope that the outcome is different this time. By all accounts Salop played well but without reward at mighty Luton, so being against another higher class team should not matter.

Apart from the vote by professional footballers in favour of possible strike action, other football news from outside the Club includes the qualification of Germany, Brazil and Ireland for the World Cup. In terms of population size the Irish feat is the greatest. They may not be overflowing with technically gifted players but there is a spirit that other nations must envy.

The news at the Town includes the snippet that Kevin Ratcliffe admits he is interested in Rochdale's David Flitcroft. This is probably not unconnected to the possibility that half of Salop's midfield could end up in gaol if things go against them (yes, that's "gaol" not "goal"). Flitcroft was at Chester with Ratcliffe which is a good sign in that there will already be a relationship there and he would be a known quantity.

Saturday 24th November, 2001

"We threw our dice into the ring and turned up trumps." – Gregor Rioch's Dad, Bruce

Southend United (home); Football League Division Three

Previous record in league games:					
	Home			Away	
Win	Draw	Lose	Win	Draw	Lose
9	6	7	3	5	14

2-0 (HT 1-0); N.Jemson (40), G.Rioch (58)
Attendance: 3,452
Standpoint: In pretty much the identical spot as for the previous match.

We are out of the Cup (all cups to be precise – except the Shropshire Senior Cup) and lost away to Luton. According to report we played well in both of these games but without the rub of the green, the fall of the dice, the bounce of the ball, the kiss of Lady Luck. On Tuesday away at Carlisle, although we secured three points courtesy of a Jemson goal, the game was appalling. We were also less than convincing this afternoon, yet we scored twice and won comfortably in the end. Is it better to win than to play well? Ideally one might wish for both, but in a competitive world the final score is what is all important (though as a neutral I'd rather watch West Ham than Arsenal). Perhaps it bodes well that Salop has started to collect points regardless of the quality of the football played.

Southend arrived hoping not to extend a string of six away defeats. They played with great organisation and some resolve. They may be short of any particularly match winning players at present, but as a team they have a very physical presence, with a line-up that includes half a dozen extremely tall men. Luke Rodgers and Nigel Jemson were dwarfed once more.

Jamie Tolley and Sam Aiston are back for their first home games after injury (both played at Carlisle too) and Matt Redmile returns after suspension having missed the delights of the Brighton-Carlisle double. Andrew Tretton has apparently played well for the past three games but unfortunately for him is still considered behind Redmile and Heathcote in the central defender pecking order. Mark Atkins and

Steve Jagielka are also back in the side after being left out of the starting line-up on Tuesday. All this meant places on the bench for Karl Murray, Darren Moss, Ryan Lowe and Peter Wilding as well as Tretton. No goalkeeper was named, so presumably Peter Wilding would have taken over if something had happened to Dunbavin. Incidentally, Chris Freestone has been released by the Club, because apart from in pre-season friendlies he has rarely looked like scoring any goals; according to the Internet, Swansea City are interested in him. There is also nothing concrete about Mr Flitcroft, although the Rochdale website appears to be suggesting that he will not be leaving there.

As it turned out Darren Moss played most of the match as Jagielka was crocked during the first half. It was a first half that could have gone either way. Luke Rodgers ballooned his only chance but that was nothing compared to the shooting from Southend. They had at least three open goals but failed to hit the target. One poor man hit the right-hand goalpost and then hit the left-hand post when the ball came back to him. Unfortunately for him Salop were ahead only a minute or so later when Nigel Jemson flicked a neat backwards header in from a corner kick. Jemmo's celebrations apparently involved some by-play with a member of the crowd who had been abusing him. He would later make a public apology for this. What a shame that his tormentor should feel under no obligation to apologise.

My half-time coffee came sweetened by sugar from a sachet bearing testament to James Watt. Luckily Salop had not entirely run out of steam. The second half was a little more distinguished in terms of quality football. Town's second goal from Greg Rioch was alone worth the admission. From a set piece which had resulted from a foul on Tolley fifteen yards or so outside the box, the ball was laid off to Rioch who scorched a low drive just inside the right post. He impresses more and more.

The referee had a curate's egg of a game. He played good advantage a couple of times and didn't even reach for his cards when there was a bit of handbagging going on. I've seen referees that would have dismissed both players in such circumstances, but he separated them out from the mob, calmed them down and confined himself to a lecture. His general manner of handling the game was to be firm but approachable. I even thought I heard him calling Leon Drysdale by his Christian name – which apparent matiness did not, however, prevent him from booking Leon later in the game. Having said these positive things, there were occasions when he didn't get it quite right and when he should have taken more definite action.

The prize for the afternoon's most memorable comment goes to the Southend fans who had the good humour to render self-deprecatingly: "Sing when we're losing, we only sing when we're losing".

A Large Scotch was on sale today. At the last game they said it had been withheld but gave no reason. The fanzine's own account is that it had originally contained an article that would have offended Jake King. Either they were worried about being sued for libel or they're going soft as they get older. Maybe too it's part of the ambivalent attitude that Salop fans have towards Jake. He was revered as captain of the team that gained promotion to the old Second Division, but his term as manager was inglorious despite the blood, sweat, tears and love that he put into it – and he is in his second spell as manager of Telford. One should probably applaud the decision not to cause unnecessary offence to someone who does not deserve it. The fanzine itself has matured in other ways and is less like a student rag-mag. It still treads the path of self-indulgence (though who am I to criticise anyone for that), but there are fewer gratuitous obscenities and the spelling has improved immeasurably (English teachers notice these things).

The matchday programme this year is probably as good as it's been for a long time. I particularly like the "Whatever happened to the Town team of 19.." feature, as I have watched most of them play. Simon Shakeshaft also seems to be a find. I don't know what he's like as a physio (though he does have impressive qualifications and a nice manner with the crowd), but his contributions in the programme are usually worth reading. On the subject of Mr Shakeshaft, when he first arrived at the Club in October 2000 he was introduced in the programme as "Steve"; quite appropriate for someone who delights in the non-stop supply of solecisms around the football club.

Snippets through the week

"Football today, it's like a game of chess. It's all about money." – Radio 5 Live

According to the Blue-and-Amber website the Gay Meadow is to be purchased by Alaska. I wonder if they'll pay more for it than the USA paid Russia for Alaska ($7,200,000). – All right, I know Alaska's a property development group.

The news on Mr Flitcroft appears to have gone cold. However, rumours are now rife that Ian Stevens might be making a return to the Meadow. (As he scores for Carlisle on Saturday, this too is probably less than likely for the moment.) I wonder whether general knowledge of this sort of behind-the-scenes activity is inevitably greater given the growth of the Internet.

I had coffee in the players' lounge at Villa Park today, followed by a meeting in the room where they probably do their TV interviews – it had that collage of logos on the wall that is always used as the background for Premiership interviews. The entire suite was very smart, not to say plush. The carpet had a rather fetching AV motif and claret and blue were ubiquitous, even on tiles in the toilet. They have spent millions on rebuilding and refurbishing the ground. This was not before time, as the main impression I got when last I ventured there (during the brief reign of Graham Turner) was of rusting girders, peeling paint, grime and decay. – Sounds familiar?

I hear on the radio that the cosy non-league set-up at Bridgnorth that I was extolling earlier has suffered something of a seismic shock. They have not only lost their manager and coach, but half their playing squad have followed them. Several aspects of this appear somewhat irregular and there will no doubt be further developments (which will include former Town player, Paul Tester, becoming manager) .

George Harrison has sadly died. After *The Beatles* broke up he released an album with the title "All Things Must Pass". This surely offers irrefutable evidence that he never witnessed the Salop midfield on a bad day.

All-time Salop Favourites Number Six – Gerry Daly

"And he crosses the line with the ball almost mesmerically tied to his foot with a ball of string..." – Ian Darke

Gerry Daly, who must surely tire of jokes about German newspapers (so let's pretend I haven't mentioned it, eh Gerry?), was a player of genuine class; he was undoubtedly one of the greatest players to grace the Meadow – and that includes visiting teams. He may not have won many balls in midfield through his tackling but the accuracy of his passing was breathtaking. This Irish wizard moved gracefully and with ease, comfortable with the ball and confident when distributing it. So much in control was he that he seemed not to break sweat, though this was deceptive as his work-rate was extremely high. It was not for nothing that he won 46 Caps for the Republic of Ireland.

My first view of him at Shrewsbury was of him not actually playing. When he first arrived he didn't play straightaway – possibly he was suspended. Instead he turned up to watch, looking very stylish in a long overcoat. And style was very much a key word as far as Gerry Daly was concerned.

He was born in Cabra, Dublin in April 1954 and started his playing career with Dublin-based Bohemians. In April 1973 Manchester United signed him for a mere £20,000. He made almost 140 appearances for United, including 107 in the League, and scored 32 goals (23 in the League), but did not stay as long as his talent suggested he would. In March 1977 he moved to Derby County for £175,000. In three and a half years there he played 111 League games, scoring 31 goals, and had a loan spell with the wonderfully named New England Tea Men. In August 1980 he joined Coventry City where he played 82 League games (15 goals) in four years. Whilst there he was loaned to Leicester City for whom he played some 17 games during 1983. In August 1984 he was on the move once more, this time to Birmingham City.

He was at Birmingham for just a year (31 league games), before coming to Salop in October 1985. He played a relatively small number of games for us too, but mere length of service is not one of the criteria I have used for choosing the players I have featured in more detail. Gerry Daly played just 65 games, including 55 in the League, and scored 8 goals.

After his stint with Salop he was off to Stoke City (in March 1987, for £15,000) where he played 17 league games (1 goal). In July 1988 he went on a free transfer to Doncaster Rovers, playing 37 league games (4 goals). In December 1989 he became assistant player manager at Telford United, and was manager from July 1990 until 1993.

It is the tale of a wandering soul. Gerry Daly's career contained more clubs than a caddie handles, including eight English League clubs. He outstayed his welcome nowhere, but left many football fans with fond memories.

Saturday 1st December, 2001

"Unfortunately, we keep kicking ourselves in the foot." – Ray Wilkins

Exeter City (home); Football League Division Three

Previous record in league games:					
Home			Away		
Win	Draw	Lose	Win	Draw	Lose
9	6	4	5	4	10

0-1 (HT 0-1)
Attendance: 3,565
Standpoint: Ditto last match.

The morning was drab, cold and exceedingly wet. The rain persisted so long that one wondered about the possibility of games near rivers needing to be postponed. The Severn was actually washing over the footpath where it runs under the English Bridge and heads off in the direction of the Gaol. People were still using the path, so football still seemed a possibility. By sunset the skies had cleared to such an extent that the full moon was a constant companion as I drove back to Birmingham.

And the game? Oh, yes; the game.

A charitable epithet would be undistinguished. A more frank description would be nondescript, if that is not a contradiction in terms. The fact that Ian Dunbavin (with a couple of saves that were both brave and technically excellent) was the best Salop player on the day tells its own story. The rest of the team was a unit that did not function together. It was a car without oil in the engine. A student who has been unkindly dragged from bed for a nine o'clock lecture. A brain the morning after a lobotomy. Rodgers and Jemson never looked like the most potent scoring duo in the division, mainly because they had no service whatsoever and the Exeter defence was well marshalled. The midfield showed itself to be lacking in ideas. The defence was relatively solid, except for the odd occasion such as when Mick Heathcote put the ball out for a throw-in when he should have done better; this might not have mattered except that nobody bothered to mark the Exeter players who accepted the invitation and proceeded to score. Thereafter it was a matter of Town trying to penetrate Exeter's defensive wall. The simple truth is that they struggled to make any impact against a team that maintained its shape and organisation.

There was one particular weak spot in the defence. Iain Jenkins, standing in for the suspended Leon Drysdale, has just been transfer-listed. His performance today will not draw many covetous chairmen waving cheque-books. His distribution was wayward, consistently finding the opposition or the crowd in preference to a team-mate. One appalling attempt at a tackle led to Mick Heathcote getting booked as he tried to remedy the resultant situation. I have just done the picture-caption competition on the Blue-and-Amber website. The prize is Iain Jenkins's shirt from last year. There would be a certain irony if I were to win! Incidentally, the picture was of Town conceding one of four goals to Rochdale at home last season. My caption, referring rather obviously to what happened in the away game was: "Don't panic, lads. We'll just drop Peer and stuff them in the away game."

Sam Aiston continues to prove Sunderland right in letting him go. He might have speed and the ability to get round his marker, but, even if he evades this man (and the extra marker some teams employ), he just cannot provide a cross that is of any use at all. Has anyone on the coaching staff of any club ever bothered to work on this with him? With a little of David Beckham's dedication to practice, he might one day become a valuable asset, but....

The referee had an average game. He proved to be fond of waving yellow cards, but fortunately didn't manage to graduate to red. He also suffered a special form of blindness that meant he was incapable of seeing when a hand touched the ball. The scorer of the goal appeared to require only one hand to control the ball, so that was fair enough. How the black-suited official managed to award a goal-kick when the Exeter goalkeeper palmed out Luke Rodgers's goal bound shot, however, will forever remain a mystery.

But, hey – we're still sixth in the table. It could be worse.

The Festive Season

"It's like a big Christmas pudding out there." – Don Howe

Not a lot of football-related action this week as Salop are no longer in the Cup. There are more rumblings about the New Meadow, or at least with agreements about what might happen to the Gay Meadow. This news was overshadowed in the short term by the signing of the manager's mate, Big Nev, formerly variously referred to (mostly by the Welsh) as the greatest goalkeeper in the world, or (by Everton fans) as the greatest goalkeeper in Europe, or (by Liverpool fans) as the fourth best keeper in Liverpool. Mr Southall is now in his forties, and the scales possibly show him still to be great, but he is considered good enough as a standby in case anything should happen to Ian Dunbavin. It might be interesting to see a legend in action, but it is probably better to pray for the continued health and prosperity of Mr Dunbavin.

There was a brief bit on *Midlands Today* focusing on the signing of Neville Southall and showing the Town in training. Big Nev looked flexible enough, in a roly-poly sort of way, but (joking aside) he would be a safer bet between the posts than some. He will be on the bench on Saturday, and, if he should play, would smash out of sight the previous record for the oldest player to represent Salop (currently held by Asa Hartford, at 40 years and 2 months).

In the event it was not Big Nev who was destined to hit the goal-keeping headlines in the game at Halifax. Ian Dunbavin threatened to monopolise the tabloid space with a couple of crucial saves, but the Halifax keeper who was playing his first game selfishly stole the limelight by getting himself sent off by upending Rory Fallon (a young striker currently on loan from Barnsley). This latter gentleman was playing courtesy of Nigel Jemson's suspension for collecting an impressive array of yellow cards. The fans on the Blue-&-Amber website had voted Mick Heathcote as their nomination for stand-in skipper, but the job had been handed to Mark Atkins. The extra responsibility must have had an effect, because he scored both of Town's goals (including the penalty which Jemmo would have taken had he been there) in the 2-1 victory.

I have started to watch *Meadow Memories.* I cannot recommend this enough to any Town fan. Highlight so far for me has been Peter

Dolby's account of fitting in a full day's work, cycling to the Meadow, scoring his two goals against Everton, and then getting up early for work the next morning. – Players these days! They don't know they're born.

Neville Southall has set a record, but it's not that for being the oldest player to represent Salop in a competitive game. Instead it's for one of the shortest stays at the club ever. He has scarcely had time to warm up his spot on the subs' bench when he is off to become manager of Dover, or somewhere of a similar ilk. All the best, Nev.

Salop now seem to be going through a non-productive patch. I missed the Macclesfield game because I was swapping Salop for salopettes and had to be out of my bed at some ungodly hour on Saturday morning. I kept in touch via Ceefax and thought it might have been a typical tale of woe when Macclesfield went ahead. It was good that Luke Rodgers finally ended his lean run and settled the affair at 1-1. Still in the potential play-off spots as the Christmas programme gets underway.

To make up for my lack of football reportage over the festive season, here is an appropriate crossword...

Clues

Across

2. ___ Meadow

4. An unlucky shot might hit this.
5. More appropriate for Easter than Christmas?
7. ___ Through the Night
8. Where we all live
11. Tony _____, whose appearances as a Town full-back were mostly in 1969.
15. Shrewsbury, Shropshire or a French dirty old man
17. A midfielder who played for Town 1967-71. Also his son, currently rated at over a million.
18. One end of the Gay Meadow.
20. Paul Edwards.

Down

1. One of Town's Scottish managers
2. ______ Turner
3. A slight improvement on seeing red
4. Prevent from entering
6. An alternative to electricity for cooking the turkey
9. Headless champions, a unit of electric current
10. Russian king
12. Precious stone
13. Enthusiastic and sounding like a Manchester United player
14. ___ Wood
16. The result of a red card
19. Britain hasn't had one for about fifty years; Christmas has three of them; the Town have had one, who has been with us twice.

Now try this party game. Match the person to the New Year's Resolution. To make it more difficult (or possibly more easy) there are more resolutions than people.

For those who want to check/cheat, the solutions to both puzzles are somewhere at the end of the book.

A. Sam Aiston
B. Nigel Jemson

C. Malcolm Starkey
D. Roland Wycherley
E. Luke Rodgers
F. Kevin Ratcliffe

1. I will lead Shrewsbury Town to the New Meadow.
2. I will answer correspondence immediately.
3. I will try harder.
4. When not wearing shorts, I will keep my trousers on at all times.
5. I will smile more often. – I've been told I have nice teeth.
6. I will not throw more than two toys out of the pram at the same time.
7. I will brush up on my Italian and Spanish. – You never know when they might come in handy.
8. I resolve not to hit the bar so often (or so soon).

I must reiterate how indispensable the video *Meadow Memories* is for all Salop fans. Not only is it a marvellously comprehensive coverage of the Town's history but there are many fascinating insights. It is worth it just to hear Vic Kasule's own side to his story; after watching the video I felt much greater sympathy for the man than I have taken from anything I have read about him.

Famous Shrewsbury Town Fans: Number One – Wilfred Owen
"Life was a damned muddle... a football game with everyone off-side and the referee gotten rid of." – F. Scott Fitzgerald

Wilfred Owen was arguably the greatest British poet of the Twentieth Century. He was born at Plas Wilmot, Oswestry, and lived at various times and addresses in Shrewsbury, including from 1910 onwards in Monkmoor Road, within walking distance of the Gay Meadow (although Salop did not at that time play their games there). He also attended Shrewsbury Technical School and was a pupil-teacher at a school on the Wyle Cop. His interest in football is on record and it is natural to conclude that he would have been a Salop fan. He was acquainted with Walter Forrest, an International

Footballer (see Owen's letter to his sister Mary, 8 May 1917) and admits to refereeing a Football Match (letter to his Mother, 1 July 1918). He even refers to Arthur Rowley in a letter to his Mother (January 1915: though probably not *the* Arthur Rowley, nor indeed any of the Arthur Rowleys referred to elsewhere in this book).

As Owen was immersed in the horrors of World War I, it is not surprising that few of his poems celebrate the happy or frivolous. One of his poems, "Disabled", does combine war and football. The subject of the poem [and this bit isn't a joke] is someone who had been a gifted footballer ("After the matches, carried shoulder high"), but is disabled after joining up, and on returning "Some cheered him home, but not as crowds cheer Goal". Owen's poems of course resonate with references to his home, the link being particularly strong in his "Roundel" where in a mere eleven lines "Shrewsbury Town" is mentioned three times, as well as one reference to "Salopian".

New Year's Irresolution

"We are now entering a new Millennium and football's a completely different cup of tea." – Dave Bassett

After the next two games we are remarkably still in sixth place, though the pack is closing. I was glad to be out of the country on Boxing Day; otherwise I might have been tempted to travel to Cheltenham, where we went down 0-1. The York match sounded likewise frustrating, with Town failing to despatch a poor, ailing team and Jemson getting dismissed again. A Ryan Lowe goal was only enough for one point. It might be a merciful breather that the Bristol Rovers game was called off on New Year's Day – not only called off, but sensibly far enough in advance that distant fans did not make unnecessary journeys in icy and dangerous conditions.

Would that the powers that be had been as decisive over the Oxford United game scheduled for Saturday 5th January! A pitch inspection at 1 o'clock Friday ruled it playable subject to a further inspection at 10 o'clock on Saturday morning to check that the promised thaw was having an impact. The 10 o'clock inspection still said "yes".

However, after a further inspection at 12 o'clock, the game was called off because it had been raining heavily rather than the expected drizzle. By the time this was public knowledge I was already in Shropshire, along with many more long- and medium-distance fans. Malcolm Starkey talked on Radio Shropshire about showing the pitch to convince some poor Oxford fan who had travelled up from London. I'm sure that was a great consolation to the fellow, but it wasn't to me and many others. As far as I am concerned, I have again wasted time and money and will probably not make the fixture when it is rearranged on a weekday evening, which means the Club will lose out on revenue. It is a situation in which there are unfortunately no winners, and Salop stand to be big losers – they are still footing police bills at £5,000 a time; they are losing any sort of momentum in terms of their season; and they are losing money through the turnstiles and the goodwill of supporters.

As I foretold, I did not make the Oxford game, but at least Salop won, through a Darren Moss goal. He managed to be sent off at Hartlepool, though goals from Rodgers and Murray earned a draw.

Normal service is about to be resumed for me tonight. I'm back after my (enforced) personal Winter break. The idea of British football taking a scheduled Winter break each season has the flaw that we cannot predict when the most atrocious weather will occur each year – or indeed the form it will take. Last season, for example, as well as December postponements there were November floods at the Gay Meadow and something nasty at Darlington in February. This season we have had a waterlogged pitch when we should have played Darlington at home in October, and in January a frozen pitch for the Bristol Rovers game followed immediately by another case of too much water when we should have been entertaining Oxford United. In other years it could be November fogs, March gales, January earthquakes, frogs and locusts in September.

In terms of the football Town seem to have come through a slightly rocky patch, but the immediate future represents anything but an easy path. The elevated position of fourth is not only flattering but could be blown away overnight if the pack of teams snapping at our heels win their outstanding games – for, strangely, although Salop have suffered postponements, we have still played more league games than others. There are also problems with half the players undergoing suspensions or injuries, half being pre-occupied with court-appearances, and the other half retaking GCSE Maths with me. In order to consolidate we need to do a Manchester United and start winning consistently. They have now reached the top of the Premier League for the first time this season, when a few weeks ago they were so many points off the pace that Sir Alex Ferguson was sounding more lugubrious than Sir Alex Ferguson and bookies were even offering decent odds against them winning the title. As for Salop, though a point at Hartlepool might have been a virtual victory for the past couple of seasons, this season, however, if the raised expectations of this campaign are to achieve concrete outcomes then it is two points lost.

In the programme-update for the Bristol Rovers game Kevin Ratcliffe's Team Talk insists that the Hartlepool game had not been "viscous" (sic). That was lucky I suppose, because a viscous game is just what we don't need when we're going through a sticky patch.

All-time Salop Favourites Number Seven – Paul Maguire

"They had a dozen corners, maybe twelve – I'm guessing." – Craig Brown

Without **Paul Maguire** there would not have been the famous "Shrewsbury Corner".

For those of you who missed out on this phenomenon which originated sometime in or just before the promotion season of 1978-9, this essentially involved the corner kick being aimed just short of the near post. From here it was back-headed across the goal-mouth for someone else to power in. It was very difficult to defend against for a number of reasons. The keeper could not come out to it because that would leave his goals exposed. He would thus remain in his goal-mouth where unfortunately for him he was rendered largely unsighted by the mêlée of players jumping by the near post. Nor could a defender easily snuff out the danger of the initial kick, the main reason being the critical height at which it was delivered. Any attempt to jump with the target-attacker carried the potential hazard that the ball would skid off the defender's head and effectively do the attacker's job for him. It worked brilliantly and after featuring once or twice on TV received the flattery of attempted copies by all and sundry.

As I said, Paul Maguire was vital to this cunning stratagem at Salop. It was his ability to ping the ball unerringly onto the head of one of the men standing at the near post that made the move possible. Those were wonderful days. The level of expectation whenever Salop were awarded a corner has never been equalled.

Paul Maguire was, however, much more than just a taker of deadly corner-kicks. He was a gifted dribbler, one of the best ever at the Meadow. He earned many vital free-kicks and penalties through weaving his way towards or into the box, only to be deprived of his legs by some desperate full-back.

He also bequeathed to Town fans memories of some magnificent individual performances. Prime among these is the way he saw off Manchester City (Malcolm Allison and all) on a frozen Meadow pitch in the Fourth Round of the FA Cup in January 1979. City were obviously not up for the game, but Paul Maguire skipped over the ice like Christopher Deane or John Curry. He scored one goal and put over the corner from which Sammy Chapman got the other.

Paul Maguire was born in Glasgow in August 1956 and signed for Salop twenty years later. In the four years he was with us he played 143 League games (plus 8 as sub) in which he scored thirty-five goals. He netted another twenty-two in 42 other appearances in sundry cup competitions. The number of goals he scored is, however, a limited guide to his value to the team; he possibly provided a higher proportion of assists per games played than anyone who has represented Salop. He moved on in September 1980 to Stoke City for the princely sum of £262,000. He probably did not have the time at the top that his talents deserved. He was the target of some pretty tough tackling and I seem to remember he had problems with his back. In five seasons at Stoke he played 93 league games, scoring 24 goals. As well as Stoke he played at Port Vale, where he scored 22 times in 101 league outings. He also went abroad to such exotic sounding teams as Braga (nine matches but no goals in 1984) and Tacoma Stars.

The layperson's guide to football terminology – Number 4

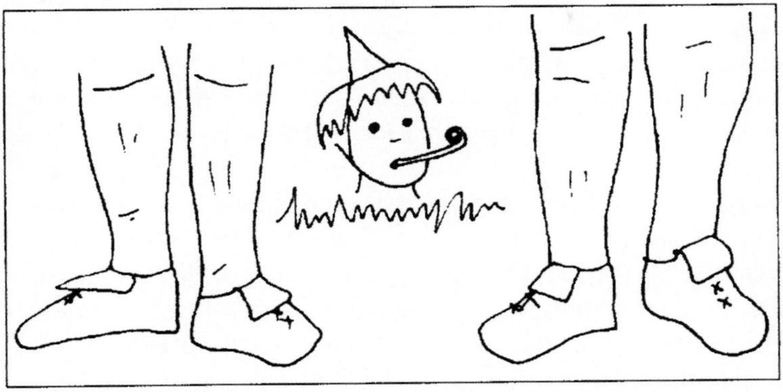

"He played in the hole behind the front two."

Tuesday 15th January, 2002
"They have missed so many chances they must be wringing their heads in shame." – Ron Greenwood

Bristol Rovers (home); Football League Division Three

Previous record in league games:					
Home			Away		
Win	Draw	Lose	Win	Draw	Lose
10	4	6	2	5	14

0-1 (HT 0-0)
Attendance: 3,475
Standpoint: On the Riverside against a barrier between the penalty

area and the half-way line in the Station End half.

From the Salop point of view it was a brilliant first half, lacking only the goals. There was wave upon wave of Shrewsbury attacking, several corners and usefully placed free kicks, and a number of impressively flowing passing movements. All, however, came to nothing; Luke Rodgers hit the post, but we should have had the game sewn up by half-time. Bristol's current hot-shot, Nathan Ellington, looked fast but he was mostly kept in check or did not finish well.

A different game in the second half. It was as though there was an unspoken rule that only the team kicking towards the Station End was allowed to attack. Kevin Ratcliffe's half-time reorganisation at Hartlepool of the ten-man team has been rightly praised as showing his tactical astuteness. He could not have known the extent to which the team needed extra inspiration at half-time today, nor is it likely that he instructed them to play the ball in the air rather than to feet.

The performance and fortunes of Salop were mirrored in those of Sam Aiston. In the first half he was full of running and frightened the Bristol defence (they were not to know that he could neither cross a ball nor pass it accurately if his life depended on it). In the second half he was ineffectual and merely managed to get booked twice and dismissed a few minutes before Town conceded the game's only goal just at the death.

At the end the only claim that Salop could have to class was that Steve Jagielka had come on, and "Jagielka" rhymes with "Anelka". He had replaced loan-player Rory Fallon, of whom it was my first view. Fallon's stature and gait are not unlike those of Ruud van Nistlerooy. He also looks as if he aspires to copy the Dutchman's hairstyle. – A pity he never looked to have any of the United player's predatory instincts in front of goal.

Bristol meanwhile had brought on veteran Mark Walters, who began as a precocious talent at Villa Park, having been born in Aston. Is it sad to see someone who has played for the likes of Villa, Glasgow Rangers and Liverpool now coming on as a sub in Third Division football or is it nice that he should still retain the desire to keep playing? Bristol also have David Hillier, whom I remember playing for Arsenal.

I read two different reasons for Salop losing, both attributed to Kevin Ratcliffe. One was that they were tired and ran out of steam. Considering that there is no additional pressure for Salop from cup games, that the opposition had also played at the weekend (though maybe they didn't travel so far or indulge in extra-curricular activities), that modern professional footballers are supposed to be fit, that squad rotation and substitution are options, and that it is not the end of the season, many would afford limited credence to this excuse. However, given the Salop habit this season of using only ten men when eleven are permitted, it is little wonder that tiredness might occasionally creep in. The other justification offered was that the sending off occurred at a crucial moment. Is this another – coded – way of expressing that his patience with Sam Aiston is running very low?

Saturday 19th January, 2002

"In comparison, there's no comparison." – Ron Greenwood

Plymouth Argyle (home) ; Football League Division Three

Previous record in league games:					
Home			Away		
Win	Draw	Lose	Win	Draw	Lose
11	5	3	2	10	8

3-1 (HT 1-1); Rodgers (44), Aiston (50), Lowe (84)
Attendance: 4,796
Standpoint: During the first half on the Riverside, level with the penalty area at the Wakeman End; second half, about ten yards away from the goal-line at the Station End.

Picture this: a team that was dead on its legs during the second half of the game on Tuesday; the opposition are running away with the

Third Division title; after five minutes Plymouth are ahead courtesy of a cruel deflection which gives Ian Dunbavin no chance; after 15 minutes Town are reduced to ten men when Gregor Rioch is dismissed following his second innocuous trip on a Plymouth player. What should be the outcome of this game? – Humiliation for Salop? A game that descends into anarchy and acrimony? A field-day for the moaners in the crowd? Any and all of these were quite likely.

And what does happen? The sheer awfulness of the refereeing fires up the crowd and galvanises the Town players into producing the home performance of the season. Until the sending off Town had been second best; Plymouth were looking good and were enjoying all the luck. However, what at first seemed to be the ultimate in ill fortune strangely proved to be the catalyst for a remarkable transformation. With their backs to the wall and urged on by a vocal and supportive crowd, Salop gradually grew in belief and not only performed brilliantly as individuals but also played for each other in a way that rarely happens.

The team was reorganised so that at first Ryan Lowe dropped back to fill the left-back slot vacated by Rioch; then new loan-player Andy Thompson (ex-Wolves) came on in place of Rory Fallon. At this point there had almost been a crucial decision that would have given the game an entirely different outcome. The number that went up on the substitution board was that of Ryan Lowe, not Fallon. If Ryan Lowe had gone off, I am not sure that the Town's performance would have reached such heights. Thompson went to left-back and Lowe went to play up to front with Rodgers, where he produced the performance of his life. He was full of running; he was provider for the first two goals and scored the third; he was truly magnificent, inspired and inspirational.

The timing of the Town goals was also a crucial matter. The first, a terrific psychological blow delivered by Luke Rodgers, came just before half-time and thus sent them off to the break not only level but on a high. The second (scored by villain-turned-hero, Sam Aiston, just five minutes after the break) settled them into the second half. The third, just reward for Ryan Lowe, killed off any fight that Plymouth might have had. They had virtually given up making much of an effort after being embarrassed to be awarded such an unfair and undeserved advantage by the referee. Maybe they thought it was all too easy and the game was already won. As time went on, however, they were to grow frustrated and embarrassed at being given the run-around by ten-man Shrewsbury for the second time in a season. They found that the referee was not totally one-sided when he ruled out their claims for an equaliser and even had Michael Evans, their goalscorer, booked (it didn't seem to be for anything more than clumsiness, though I later read it was for dissent).

In contrast, the Town players grew in belief as the game progressed. Football is in the head and heart as much as in the legs and lungs. Luke Rodgers was back to his lively best; one attempt he made to chip the goalkeeper from forty yards would have been goal of the season if Larrieu had not been alert. Jamie Tolley was magnificent in midfield and looks to be a commanding presence for many years (if he stays, that is). Mark Atkins played what I thought was his best game for Salop. From Dunbavin to Aiston they played their part.

Those not actually on the pitch also had considerable influence. Kevin Ratcliffe once more showed sound command of strategy. Not only did he get the immediate reorganisation right in the first half, but withdrawing scorer Sam Aiston to bolster the middle of the defence with Peter Wilding was also a shrewd move during the endgame. The crowd, who had played a not inconsiderable part in the proceedings, were singing "We only need ten men" out of conviction not bravado. This was ultimately the game that you turn up throughout the season hoping to see on every occasion but are grateful that it happens at least once.

Plymouth will not want to play Salop too often, but I suspect that this defeat will not unduly retard their promotion push. Town on the other hands will welcome the three points.

In football the link between the past and the present is never far away, as witnessed by this pre-match banter:
"The last time I came here Paul Maguire was playing."
"He's playing today."

My half-time sugar sachet bore the image of Harry Houdini. (Only joking.)

All-time Salop Favourites Number Eight – Oggy

"I was saying the other day, how often the most vulnerable area for goalies is between their legs…" – Andy Gray

Shrewsbury Town have had some great goalkeepers – Russell Crossley, Alan Humphreys, Alan Boswell, John Phillips, Ken Mulhearn, Bob Wardle. The greatest, however, in my opinion (and also according to a recent poll on the Blue-and-Amber website) has to be **Steve Ogrizovic**, inevitably and affectionately known as Oggy.

Not to be confused with Zoran Ogrizovic (a Croatian midfielder), Steven Ogrizovic was born in Mansfield in September, 1957. As a goalkeeper, Oggy was a giant who dominated his area and filled his goals with a presence more than physical. He was so tall (seeming much taller than his official height of 6' 5") and athletic that forwards stood little chance with high balls into his area. Narrowing angles was a speciality and I still have visions of Oggy flashing horizontally across the goal-mouth.

Oggy's record at Shrewsbury speaks for itself. He spent only two seasons at Salop, but in that brief spell established himself as something of a legend. It must be remembered that his time at Salop corresponded with our visit to the old Second Division and more precisely with two of our three highest ever placings; that is, ninth in 1982-3 and eighth in 1983-4 (we repeated eighth position in 1984-5, but after that things slid a little....).

Oggy came to Salop from Liverpool in 1982 in some sort of exchange deal with Bob Wardle. He had managed only four league appearances in almost five years at Liverpool and had presumably tired of being permanent understudy first to Ray Clemence and then to Bruce Grobbelaar. Prior to Liverpool, he had been with Chesterfield, for whom he made sixteen league appearances, having joined them July 1977.

In 1984 Oggy left Salop (for a fee of £82,000) to serve Coventry City, where his performances not only put him on the fringe of an

England squad whose goalkeeping was still dominated by Messrs Shilton and Clemence, but were also undoubtedly a key factor in Coventry's repeated defiance of the odds in maintaining their existence in the top division. Oggy actually holds the record for most appearances for Coventry, some 600 (including 507 League appearances) and the record for consecutive league appearances (209 games between 1984 and 1989). He even managed that rare feat for a goalkeeper of scoring a goal; this came in the away match against Sheffield Wednesday on the 25th October, 1986. The highlight of his career, however, must have been winning the FA Cup with Coventry in 1988. After a long and distinguished career he finally decided to hang up his gloves at the end of the 1999-2000 season and has since been a coach with Coventry (and even had a match in charge after Roland Neilson was sacked).

As well as the rewards that he has gained directly from his efforts on the field Oggy has picked up a good share of awards. These include several Coventry Player of the Year type awards and a prize from the Football Writer's Association. The most prestigious, however, must be the Professional Footballers' Association merit award that he received in 1998. A look at the list of others to be similarly honoured in other years reveals what an honour this bestows. The catalogue includes: Pele, Bill Shankly, Bob Paisley, Joe Mercer, Brian Clough, Gordan Strachan, Sir Stanley Matthews, Sir Bobby Charlton, Denis Law and Nat Lofthouse. – Distinguished company indeed.

Oggy was the consummate professional who is reported to have been clapped by his Coventry team-mates when Gordan Strachan announced that it was his 600th first class game (or something of the like). One of his chief assets was that he maintained a wonderful level of fitness and avoided injury almost miraculously for a goalkeeper – or maybe it is truer to say that whatever injury he received was shrugged off stoically rather than that it was avoided entirely. He overcame the setback of a broken leg in 1995 and the odd broken nose or two. There were several seasons, including his two at Salop, when he was an ever-present in the team and he was still playing at the age of 42. These facts alone, fairly remarkable in the modern era, testify to his fitness, endurance and love of the game. He was an all-round sportsman who when not between the sticks was playing snooker or bowling (right arm medium fast) and batting for Shrewsbury Cricket Club. He even played in Minor Counties matches for Shropshire, including four List A games (NatWest Trophy) in 1983-4, scoring 23 runs at an average of 11.5, making one catch, and taking five wickets off 39 overs at an average of 28.2. His victims included Yorkshire and England's Martin Moxon and Warwickshire and West Indies player Alvin Kallicheran. He must have been very disappointed that, because of football commitments, he missed Shrewsbury's trip to Lords, and with it the rare double of competing at both Wembley and Lords. Still, his bat made the journey and was used by a team-mate on his behalf (possibly, as my brother suggests, scoring the winning six off the last ball of the last over – though his memory may be over-romanticising here).

The Oggy Interview

As well as being a great goalkeeper, Steve Ogrizovic proves to be not only a gentleman who gives willingly of his time to nuts like me but also still passionate about football and a bit of a Shrewsbury fan.

ALAN: What sort of memories have you got of your time at Shrewsbury?

STEVE: Thoroughly enjoyable ones. It's a great place to live and I thoroughly enjoyed my football. I'd come down from Liverpool – Graham Turner bought me, giving me the chance to play first team football in the old second division. I thought at the time we had a young under-rated team that had it stayed together could probably have gone on to even better things. There were a lot of players in that side who actually went on and played at a higher level – Ross McLaren, Steve Cross, Nigel Pearson, Bernard McNally – there were a lot of good players. I think Graham Turner did well actually getting together such a good group of young players. My recollection is of just walking into a team that had a good team-spirit; there was a rapport between players and I had a terrific two years. I really enjoyed it, both on and off the pitch. Gay Meadow is probably not the place that most people associate with top football teams but I certainly enjoyed it there. It was a good team, and the fans and the atmosphere at the Gay Meadow were very good then as well.

ALAN: You actually lived in Shrewsbury didn't you?

STEVE: I did do. I lived just opposite the cricket ground.

ALAN: Have you retained any links with Salop?

STEVE: It's difficult really when you move away. I still talk to or see quite a few of those I played cricket with. I've not seen Ken Mulhearn for a few years, but we used to speak quite often. Quite a few of the other cricketers I played with I have kept in touch with. But the footballers all tended to move away to different clubs. That's the problem with football: not too many players stay in one place for long.

ALAN: No, not many Bobby Charltons, are there? What sort of memories have you got of those Cup games against Ipswich and the ones at Goodison Park?

STEVE: They were enormous games because they were against top teams. We beat Ipswich. Shrewsbury were renowned for being a very good Cup side before I came. I remember we beat Ipswich 2-0 at Gay Meadow. Ipswich were a decent First Division side at the time, but we fancied our chances. We were at home and like I say there was a good Cup tradition. We played very well and it was one of the biggest games we played. And it was the same when we went to play at Everton. Everton were one of the top teams in the First Division at the time – they may have won the Championship around then. They were very strong and unfortunately we played at Goodison Park. Had it been at Gay Meadow we may have had a chance of a Cup upset, but it was asking a lot at Goodison Park. We went up there twice in two years, didn't we? – they won 2-1 and 3-0, I think.

ALAN: Yes, and for the first game you had to do without Bernard McNally.

STEVE: That's right, he couldn't play on a Sunday. I think we acquitted ourselves quite well. We were never good enough to beat them but gave it our best shot.

ALAN: What sort of reflections have you got on your own career? What would you say was the highpoint?

STEVE: I'd have to say winning the FA Cup when I was at Coventry. I was quite ambitious, as I think most footballers are. I wanted to play at the top and went to Coventry to play football in the top division. It was an opportunity I couldn't really turn down. I've enjoyed a wonderful career at Coventry, culminating in the success of '87-8.

ALAN: Do you think that goalkeepers are at all different from other players? It's sometimes said that goalkeepers are mad.

STEVE: I don't think they're mad. I think they have to be more resilient. As a goalkeeper you're an individual. You've got to have broad shoulders. You've got to be very thick skinned for the simple reason that if a goalkeeper has a bad game everyone knows about it. If a striker, midfield player or a defender has a bad game they're not always punished, but the poor goalkeeper often is. So you have to be thick skinned, you have to be very resilient. You have to be prepared to put setbacks behind you very quickly. You're not going to last long as a goalkeeper if you can't do that. – Whereas outfield players can overcome such situations quickly because their mistakes aren't quite so serious.

ALAN: Would you encourage a son or a nephew to become a professional footballer?

STEVE: I certainly would. If they've got the talent. Especially the way football is now. Football is even more high profile and fashionable than ever. Anybody who's sports minded always wants to be a professional footballer. The rewards are there for anyone who does well. Top players are millionaires now, unlike a few years ago.

ALAN: Do you think that football actually looks after footballers? — the ones who perhaps aren't quite so fortunate

STEVE: We've got a very strong union, the PFA. I think the PFA does as much as it possibly can to look after the footballers. As for clubs, unfortunately it's like everything else, the players are sometimes regarded by football clubs as just part of the rolling stock and it's possible that some clubs could look after the players a little bit better. I can only speak from personal experience. I feel I've always had a very good relationship with the clubs I've played with. After I finished my playing career at Coventry I carried on coaching. I would say that clubs generally do look after the players. They've looked after me, although perhaps I should add that I know other players who might say that their experience has been otherwise.

ALAN: Thanks very much for your time.

STEVE: No problem, and good luck with the book. Do you watch Shrewsbury now regularly?

ALAN: I go fairly regularly. Part of what I'm doing in my writing is covering this season. It could go very well, depending on the next few results.

STEVE: I still look out for them. I still watch to see how they've got on. We'll keep our fingers crossed that they go up this year.

Tuesday 22nd January, 2002
"Football's not like an electric light. You can't just flick the switch and change from quick to slow." – John Greig

Macclesfield Town (away); Football League Division Three

Previous record in league games:					
Home			Away		
Win	Draw	Lose	Win	Draw	Lose
1	2	1	0	0	3

1-2 (HT 1-2); Rodgers (40)
Attendance: 1,688
Standpoint: Sitting among away supporters in a very new stand at the side of the pitch.

This was the first away game of the season that I've managed to attend. Now that we don't play Birmingham, West Brom, Villa, Wolves, Derby, Stoke, or even Walsall on a regular basis it's not been too easy to get to away games.

It was also only the second time ever that I had travelled on a football supporters' coach, and the first for some thirty-odd years. This was a somewhat different experience from that first time. Then I had travelled on a coach, with a mainly youthful and exceedingly loud group, to see Salop play Chester in a League Cup game. We had journeyed in hope and were not a little miffed when the hefty boot of Dave Pountney had scored the winner, particularly as that proud Salopian had only recently joined Chester from the Town. On the return journey, due to popular demand, the coach had stopped in Wrexham. While most partook of the delicacies at the nearest chip shop I took the opportunity to pay a rare visit to my Dad's sister, who happened to live nearby. After a cup of tea and a few congenial moments spent with Aunty Eva, I hurried back to the coach, only to find that I had almost been abandoned because the party was making a hasty exit following a spot of unprovoked trouble that some of the livelier elements had caused.

That truly seemed another world when on Tuesday evening I entered a coach packed with sober, middle-aged to elderly, staid, respectable, responsible citizens. There was scarcely a child in sight and yobbos of a noisy, violent or merely beer-swilling disposition were little in evidence. This was after all transport arranged by the official supporters' club and such bodies have done much to eradicate many of the unpleasant manifestations of former times. Were it not for the sight of so many Shrewsbury Town scarves, I might almost have been setting off for a Saga holiday in Eastbourne, so peaceful and orderly was it.

The other thing that struck me forcibly was how dedicated these people were. By most standards I am a fairly committed follower of Shrewsbury Town, yet compared to many on that coach I am hardly serious, a trifler, an amateur, a make-weight. For them this is a vital matter. It is more than a hobby, it is a way of life. They will not only be jeopardising their digestive systems, depriving themselves of sleep, upsetting work arrangements, forsaking loved-ones and giving up a considerable amount of time in order to travel in the cold and dark to sit or stand in the cold and dark to watch an execrable display of football somewhere in uncharted Cheshire, but they will also be repeating the experience when they head off for Hull on Saturday. I suspect that a considerable number have not actually missed a game, home or away, for many years. I can but salute them not only for their dedication but also for their knowledge – there were conversations I heard this night that covered events in the Club's history as far back as when we entered the Football League.

Peerless among this army of devotees has been Chris Smith, who has been organising the transport to away games for countless seasons. Sadly, due to a wretched mishap involving this evening's coach (as I understand it; I was not there, because I only joined the expedition in Wellington), he had to be taken to hospital and thus missed his first away game for twenty-five years. Missing the game would probably have been more painful to him than any physical injuries. Shankly's oft-derided comment about football being more important than life or death comes to mind.

Football grounds these days have segregated areas for fans of the opposing teams. It is perhaps sad that this should be necessary. What does it say for the degree of our civilisation that we cannot stand shoulder to shoulder with supporters of another football team without someone feeling threatened or actually being attacked? As it is, the threats and abuse are now chiefly verbal, but the tribal element of the game is thus reinforced. One can, however, feel free to cheer on one's team without the inhibition of one's neighbour's disapproval. My memory is long enough for me to remember the days before segregation came about. If you travelled to an away game then, you were careful about what you said and when you said it – unless you were part of a gang working out some macho identity thing. It often came as a surprise to realise suddenly that you were not the only Salop supporter in the ground. I recall the entire section of terraces around me erupting once when we scored the only goal of a game at Crewe's Gresty Road ground. Conversely there were occasions at the Gay Meadow when larger clubs visited that you felt more like a visitor yourself because of the number and noise of the opposition fans.

The Macclesfield stadium, Moss Rose (not to be confused with David Moss, the manager), is currently under redevelopment. Builders huts are on one flank of what must have originally been the main stand and there are hoardings bearing the legend "Alfred McAlpine". Exposed man-hole covers lurk in the turf within yards of the touchline. The fence along the front of the main seating area looks wooden, basic and possibly temporary (unless they aren't going to the expense of a wall). The terraced end where the away fans stand is open to the elements – and there were a few of them this evening. The newly erected stand has that combination of concrete and bright plastic that typifies modern stadia. The soulessness of it was emphasised by the microscopic size of the crowd. We were rattling around inside there like rocks roaming the universe or frozen peas in a cannibal's cooking-pot. There was little that one might call atmosphere and that had its impact on the game; there was nothing to lift the spirits or performance of the players on a cold, windswept evening. This was such a contrast to the atmosphere at the Meadow the previous game. The one redeeming aspect of the stadium was that it offered decent toilet and refreshment facilities.

And what of the game? The fact that I have taken so long to refer to it directly probably speaks volumes. If Saturday's performance against Plymouth was like winning the World Cup, this was like losing a relegation battle in the eleventh division of the Shropshire County league. In a nutshell (or perhaps more appropriately, in a pig's bladder) this was a case of from the sublime to the b. awful, and underlines the fact that there is little point in being brilliant when defeating the best teams in the division, if you are then too tired, too disorganised, too dispirited, too lacking in motivation, or whatever, to do a proper job against the poorer opposition.

No doubt Saturday's efforts had taken their toll. Several players looked shattered and there was no coherence in the team. Maybe the fact that Macclesfield were wearing blue was one reason that Salop players kept passing to them. One opinion voiced many times by fans during and after the game was that you should not change a winning team. I don't see that as an issue in this case. What were they suggesting Kevin Ratcliffe should have done? — Put out the ten who won the game on Saturday? — Put out the eleven who had started that game? This is extremely naïve, in that formations, manpower and tactics have to be adapted to situations. Would any clear-thinking Shrewsbury fan really suggest that a player as gifted and experience as Nigel Jemson should not be picked if eligible? Nowadays football is a squad game and care also needs to be taken to protect both the young and the older members of the squad from being burnt out. The not inconsiderable question of motivation comes into it too. It is a complex and delicate affair and although I might have my opinions I am happy to admit that KR is doing an excellent job at the moment.

Salop started with Thompson playing at left-back and Rioch playing in front of him instead of Aiston; Jemson returned after his lengthy suspension in place of Fallon. We started brightly enough but the game settled into a pretty dull affair. One moment that stood out from the dross was a spectacular first goal. Unfortunately it was scored by Kyle Lightbourne for Macclesfield; he chipped the ball over Dunbavin from fully thirty five yards after about twenty five minutes. This might have stirred Salop to action but it didn't and we went further behind a few minutes later when a nicely taken free-kick was swung into the box from the left touchline. It clipped the head of a Town player and in the goalmouth mêlée it went in. The announcement claimed the goal for Priest, but it had apparently bounced off Andy Tretton for an own goal. Just after that Town did score from a rare Luke Rodgers tap in.

The second half did not unfortunately offer any better fare. Aiston came on for Rioch and looked as if he might spice matters up, but failed. Later Karl Murray replaced Ryan Lowe, who quite understandably had been a shadow of last Saturday's hero. One of the few incidents of note was Luke Rodgers being booked for retaliation. He was fouled, but nothing was given; he then sprinted after the player and fouled him. It was an example not only of the awful refereeing that doesn't adequately pick up the original offences but also of the lack of self-control that Luke must exercise if he is going to make it at a higher lever in the game.

The matchday programme was a typical offering. Interestingly the featured "match to remember" was the first-ever F.A. Trophy Final when Macclesfield defeated Telford United 2 – 0 at Wembley in 1970. I know all about that game – because I was there, which is a fact that I would not have let slip on the Shrewsbury coach or on the terraces. Salop fans do not admit to watching Telford ever, and maybe there was a certain mischief intended by the programme editor in including reference to this particular game. (Perhaps I should admit here that I also went to watch Telford return to Wembley to win the F.A. Trophy.) The Wembley game was the first time I saw Macclesfield, and also the last until they eventually joined the league. In their first season since joining in 1997 they gained immediate promotion but came straight back down and have not done a great deal apart from providing Salop with tough opposition. We have lost every away game to them and have only won the very first home game (4-3).

One aspect of the matchday programme that was unsatisfactory was the section detailing the Salop team. Mark Atkins was listed as a defender (perhaps they know something). Iain Jenkins and Chris Freestone were both included (the former also being named as number two on the team sheet) despite having departed several weeks ago. Mind you, they are still included in the "Kit Sponsors" page in the Salop matchday programme, so perhaps I shouldn't be too critical of the inaccuracies in another club's programme.

The sugar for my coffee was out of a bowl – in keeping with the anonymity of the stadium.

And for that matter, why does a boxing ring have corners?

The performance against Hull was reported to be much better than the result. It is, however, getting to the stage where results become important. Amazingly we remain within the play-off zone, but there are too many teams able to leap-frog for that to persist.

The Hull City page on Ceefax this week referred to Salop as "Welsh wannabes". I object to this on a number of counts, the least of which is that it is intended as a gratuitous insult. A "pub team plus Rodgers" is a put-down, but does display a modicum of wit. "Welsh wannabes" on the other hand is not only racist (which image football is supposed to be cleaning up, so ITV should help by not permitting such language), it is also nastily humourless and inaccurate. On a personal level (given the number of Welsh relatives that I have) I find it offensive that to be Welsh should be a term of abuse. It also saddens me that football fans should continue to hurl such petty insults. Is it not better to display positive support for your own team than to define your identity as a supporter by your hate for others? Let us at least pretend to be civilised.

Poetic Interlude Three – *Floreat Salopia*
"The deep, unutterable woe / Which none save exiles feel." – W.E. Aytoun (1813-65)

Away from its Meadow
the blue flower of Shropshire
wilts,
in football as in life.

Written sometime before 1985, but perhaps as true today as ever.

Saturday 2nd February, 2002
"Both sides have scored a couple of goals, and both sides have conceded a couple of goals." – Peter Withe

Scunthorpe United (home); Football League Division Three

Previous record in league games:					
Home			Away		
Win	Draw	Lose	Win	Draw	Lose
8	1	3	2	4	7

2-2 (HT 2-2); Jemson (9), Rodgers (12)
Attendance: 3,345
Standpoint: On the Riverside against barriers in line with the penalty area near the Station End; in the first-half a barrier in the second row (tucked further under cover because of the rain), in the second-half a barrier in the front row (for a better view).

Games between these two clubs have a fine history; yet, although Scunthorpe joined the League on the same day as Salop, we have not actually spent many seasons in the same division. Salop used to get the better of earlier encounters but Scunthorpe have evened matters up somewhat in recent years. There have also been plenty of goals scored in these games, it being not uncommon for the victor to net four or even five. With the teams currently jostling each other like a pair of footballers rising together for a high ball, the stage should thus be set for a cracking game today.

This particular encounter was interesting. It was gripping. It was as packed with surprises as a magician's hat. It was not, however, high art, nor even great football.

The first surprise was that the game should have gone ahead at all. Games have already been called off this season after a spot of drizzle somewhere in Powys; and here was the Met Office promising hurricanes, blizzards, floods and at least three ominous horsemen. The inspection at 9 o'clock on Saturday morning, however, insisted that the pitch was playable. Experiences from earlier this year, coupled with the news that several games in various locations had been postponed, engendered a degree of caution, not to say scepticism. So it was that Salop's sticky patch became not only their current unconvincing sequence but also the surface of the Gay Meadow.

The next element of surprise carried the possibility of farce. With kick-off imminent, the loud-speaker asked for a qualified referee to come forward (reminiscent of "Is there a doctor in the house?"). We were then informed that there were slight difficulties that were being resolved, but that kick-off would be delayed five minutes as a result. When the teams and officials came out it was announced that the referee was someone who was down in the programme as assistant. I've no idea what had happened to the original referee – probably swallowed the pea out of his whistle or tripped over his pile of red cards – but his substitute was probably one of the more competent black-suited gentlemen to strut on the Meadow this season.

The pitch truly was a quagmire up the middle. The ball skidded off at pace in parts, mainly near touchlines, but stuck like unwanted guests in others. It was not a pitch suited to a passing game; Salop probably suffered as a result, as we rarely come off best when playing head-tennis.

We started brightly enough, however, and were two goals up before a quarter of an hour was on the clock. In the ninth minute Ian Woan, making his debut on loan, hit a free-kick from the left and Jemmo volleyed in after a neat four-man move that also involved Lowe and Tretton. Luke Rodgers scored the second when his shot-cum-centre from the left-wing eluded everyone and sneaked inside the far post; the keeper was probably distracted by Jamie Tolley's run into the box and looked to react to him connecting rather than concentrating on the ball itself. By half-time matters were all-square after Town had proceeded to fritter away their early advantage. The first Scunthorpe goal was a munificent giveaway as the Town defence stood statically statuesque when a corner-kick came into the box. The second was slid underneath Dunbavin after Brian Quailey had not been effectively shut out by the defence.

There were no more goals in the second half but the two players for whom the game had started so well will both for different reasons want to forget its ending. There was almost a symmetry to the game in the way that the two early scorers were early leavers. Nigel Jemson left in considerable pain with what looked like a damaged collar-bone. Luke Rodgers left just afterwards as a result of a wild elbow.

Eleven red cards. It is a statistic with which it is very difficult to argue. Those who watch Salop, however, would swear that it is not a dirty team that they follow every week. A recent poll on the internet attributed the blame for the high number of red cards to referees, and, although I am not condoning violent or ungentlemanly play, I am in agreement with that. This particular dismissal was quite justified in a way that some others have not been. Having said that, there is still an element of luck involved. Luke Rodgers was unfortunate (or stupid) enough to commit his act of violence on an opponent suspended in the air in full view of the referee, the bench and the cameras. A little earlier Leon Drysdale had received an elbow in the face, but this was as he was running and was not seen by any official. There is also almost certainly some suspicion that Town now have a reputation with referees which it will be difficult to live down.

My sugar-sachet this week has the image of Mahatma Gandhi. Maybe Town's tactics after going two-nil up were based on the idea of passive resistance.

All-time Salop Favourites Number Nine – Wayne Williams

"Well, I've seen some tackles, Jonathan, but that was the ultimatum!" – Alan Mullery

Wayne Williams represents all those Shropshire boys who over the years have made it through to play football for Salop. Perhaps more than that he represents all those who as schoolboys have dreamed of playing football at the Meadow but (because of the sad fact that most of us just are not capable of playing at that level) have never managed it. Not only did Wayne make it, he was even the captain for a while and put in over two hundred League appearances, all during the Town's sojourn in the original Second Division.

Wayne Williams's birthplace is always given as Telford, but I'm pretty sure he was probably born in Crudgington after his parents moved there from next door to me at Cold Hatton. Wherever he was actually born, it happened in November 1963.

Wayne signed for the club as an apprentice on his eighteenth birthday in 1981. He replaced Carleton Leonard as right-back for the 1982-3 season. He was an ever-present for that season and made the position his own for several seasons until Ian McNeil came to prefer Richard Green. Wayne played 212 league games for Salop (plus nine as sub), scoring seven goals. He scored another four goals in almost fifty other games with us (including winning the Welsh Cup).

He was transferred to Northampton in January 1989 (having been there on loan for three games in November the previous year), thus missing out on Town's relegation to the Third Division. I can recall him saying in an interview at the time something to the effect that it would have been nice to have spent all his career at Salop but it was not to be. He was at Northampton for two and a half seasons, playing 47 league games. In 1991 he moved on to Walsall for whom he made 56 league appearances, before playing outside the League at Kidderminster Harriers and Bridgnorth.

Wayne was a direct, no nonsense player. He tackled hard, overlapped down the line on a regular basis and was always committed to the cause. These might not be the sort of virtues to make headlines on the sports pages but they'll do for me in a full-back.

Saturday 16th February, 2002
"I can see the carrot at the end of the tunnel" – Stuart Pearce

Leyton Orient (home); Football League Division Three

Previous record in league games:					
Home			Away		
Win	Draw	Lose	Win	Draw	Lose
10	5	5	4	3	14

1-0 (HT 0-0); Jagielka (50)
Attendance: 3,299
Standpoint: On the Riverside against a barrier half-way between the penalty area at the Station End and the half-way line.

Two weeks on, and a series of small crises. Failure to hold on to a valuable winning position at Darlington (despite goals from Jagielka, Rodgers and Woan). Dumped out of the play-off places by Cheltenham. Next game against Orient who are not only smarting for revenge after what Salop did to them at Brisbane Road but who are desperate for some points themselves. The Meadow again under water on the Wednesday before a game (three cheers for the fire-brigade and the ground staff). A dearth of strikers: Jemmo out injured for the rest of the season, Luke suspended for three games, Chris Freestone no longer with us, Rory Fallon returned to his club.

There were various possibilities for dealing with the last situation. The first one that Kevin tried was the last minute loan-signing of Tony Lormor, from promotion rivals Hartlepool United. He has been around for a few years and looks the part: big and burly. In fact he is reminiscent of Nigel Jemson. Unfortunately the tame header that he landed safely in the goalkeeper's arms as the conclusion to Salop's first attack was a sign of what was to come. He is just like Jemmo, but without the skill, mobility, passion and tactical awareness. Let's be charitable and say he is probably short of match practice.

The second possibility for Kevin looked more promising: for the last ten minutes he brought young Chris Murphy off the bench. He has been hailed as the next Luke Rodgers, and certainly looks nippy. The only problem is that playing alongside Lowe and Jagielka he does not offer the physical presence that Jemmo offers to Luke. We shall see.

It was one of those matches that you look back upon with regret, but which are necessary in the grand scheme. Watching the beautiful game played beautifully week after week is not a reality, certainly not in the English Third Division. There are times when a win is more important than the manner in which it is achieved. As far as Salop is concerned this was a game that most of the team played well, but the team rarely operated as a coherent unit. It is certainly an interesting blend of youth and experience at the moment, and, although there were few flowing movements, at least they were prepared to grind out a result. Maybe the quality of their football will improve when the pitch allows them to play it more on the deck.

Objectively speaking, I was sorry for Orient. They pressed the midfield for much of the game and looked sound enough at the back. They did not, however, have one serious attempt on the Salop goal. There were a few corners and a handful of long-range shots, but there was nothing to give Ian Dunbavin sleepless nights. The goal that separated the teams was the sort that you just knew was about to happen. As soon as Orient conceded an unnecessary corner I sensed that they would regret it and I was totally unsurprised when Steve Jagielka fired home from Ian Woan's corner-kick. It was the kind of luck that you have to expect when you've got yourself in the position in the table that Orient have.

I suppose it could be argued that the game went according to historical expectation, Salop having previously won ten out of nineteen encounters at the Gay Meadow. The away pattern would of course have favoured Orient. Town have won three of the last five away fixtures at Orient, but before that had only managed one win – and I am pleased to say I was there when that happened in the 1979-80 season, the only time I have ever been there. We sneaked a one-nil win, courtesy of Steve Biggins, I think.

This week's sugar sachet featured Florence Nightingale famous for easing the suffering of soldiers in the Crimean war (Crimea being well on the way to the Orient, I think). These days she could get a job as physiotherapist, easing the suffering of footballers.

Saturday 23rd February, 2002
"Football is an art more central to our culture than anything the Arts Council deigns to recognize." – Germaine Greer

Mansfield Town (home); Football League Division Three

Previous record in league games:					
Home			Away		
Win	Draw	Lose	Win	Draw	Lose
10	7	5	5	4	14

3-0 (HT 2-0); Lowe (34), Lormor (43), Woan (85)
Attendance: 4,120
Standpoint: On the Riverside against a second tier barrier near the penalty area at the Station End.

It's true. Football is a funny old game. And much of what happens depends on chance and the confidence of players. For most of the first half I could almost have believed I was watching Shrewsbury playing away from home. Mansfield were undeniably one of the best teams to have visited this season and after the first five minutes they were doing most of the attacking. However, simultaneously Mansfield's Tankard pulls a hamstring and Salop score. The pulled hamstring was not only part of the reason that Steve Jagielka was able to put in a shot which hit the "aluminium" and Ryan Lowe followed up to net, it also compelled Mansfield to reorganise. Before they had properly recovered they were hit with the old double whammy as Lormor received a beautiful pass from Woan, steadied himself and to his immense relief tucked away the ball. He looked slightly less disorientated than last week but still needs match practice.

So, having been on the rack themselves for much of the first half, Salop went in two goals ahead. Mansfield never recovered, their self-belief and will to battle were visibly drained from them. In the second-half Salop executed some nice passing movements and had at least half a dozen clear-cut chances to increase the lead (MEMO to the coaches: instruct players not to lean back when shooting). Ian Woan capped a fine game by adding the only other goal near the end.

The difference in performance by Salop between last week and this was that they were again a unit. All individuals made excellent contributions, but they also played for each other. The youngsters – Murray, Moss, Lowe, Jagielka – ran tirelessly and the old-timers used their experience well. Despite his age Mick Heathcote must be one of the best acquisitions for many years – it's a pity we lost him in the first place. Ian Woan likewise looks to have the sort of class that has not been at the Gay Meadow for a long time; his passing reminds me of Gerry Daly and his dead-ball shooting shows promise; if he continues to contribute goals too he will prove extremely valuable.

It is ironic that we have won the two games played with neither Jemson nor Rodgers, when we might have felt that things had really turned against us. Instead of falling away we are back in the play-off frame, playing with confidence, and looking forward to the challenge of two away games against teams also interested in the idea of promotion. It is remarkable too that not only was no one sent off in today's game but the referee did not even produce one yellow card for either team. For a game this season that is as rare as a Salop visit to Wembley. Does it mean that Town are suddenly no longer a dirty side (rhetorical question!)?

The wit of the Mansfield fans with "You're just a small town in Wales" was countered by the more accurate, and probably more cruel "You're just an ex-mining town".

My sugar this week was ennobled with the visage of Nelson Mandela, not only a rarity in that he is a politician one can admire but also an avid sports fan. Remember those pictures of him in a South African rugby shirt?

The Ages of Fan – Number One: The Young Lad

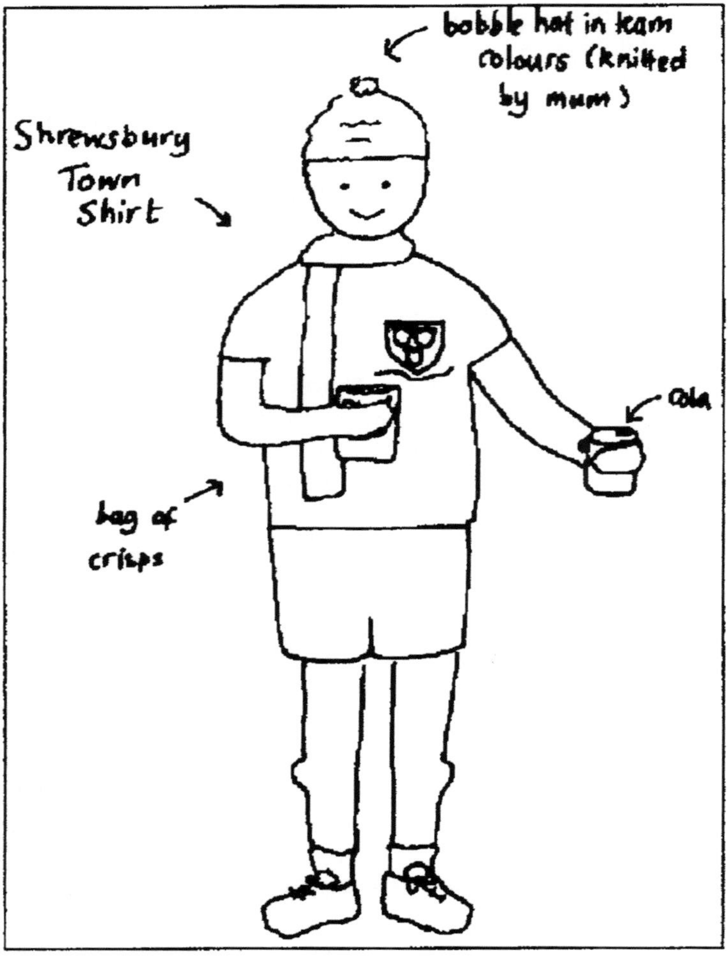

Tuesday 26th February, 2002

"Football and cookery are the two most important subjects in the country." – Delia Smith

Kidderminster Harriers (away); Football League Division Three

Previous record in league games:					
Home			Away		
Win	Draw	Lose	Win	Draw	Lose
2	0	0	0	0	1

0-1 (HT 0-1)
Attendance: 3,625
Standpoint: Sitting in the Main Stand, Row B Seat 3; that is, very near the side of the pitch, in line with the edge of a penalty area.

An evening to sort the hardened committed football fan from those that only play at it. Before the game the tail-end of last night's gale was still whisking the trees about and driving occasional horizontal sleet. It was dark as much because of the density of cloud hanging in the sky as for the late hour; though this would soon clear to leave a full moon to excite vampires, werewolves, hounds and harriers. The banks of crocus, the forsythia gold, the dangling catkins and the odd foamy blossom attest jointly to the advent of spring, but the temperature on top of the hill where the Aggborough Stadium sits contradicts that. I do not somehow think there will be a repeat of last year's unscheduled entertainment when a streaker was improvident enough to break Salop's concentration with his exhibitionism. Tonight's wind would certainly dull his ardour. Still, at least the game is unlikely to be called off because of a flooding river. Amazingly they are expecting a thousand Salop fans (and actually get the impressive figure of 1,536, which demonstrates that Salop does have a healthy sized support base).

The Kidderminster ground is of necessity modern-looking – they were denied entry to the League when they first qualified back in 1994 because their ground was not up to standard and had to wait until 2000 for a second chance. It is not a completely new stadium (à la Bescot, Pride Park, etcetera), but has been upgraded. There are obviously plans to continue this by replacing the "cowshed" on the one side of the ground, although according to the matchday programme they may even contemplate relocation at some time.

Kidderminster used to be famous for carpets. The advertising boards around the ground suggest that times have changed. One of these was for "Doolittle and Dalley". I could not see on the hoarding what these gentlemen do, but they must be either estate agents or lawyers [the former, I am reliably informed].

Radio Shropshire was heralding the match as "another make or break game for Shrewsbury Town", who would be "going for their third win in a row to cement their play-off credentials". For Kidderminster, defeat would "kill off their hopes". I suppose they have to say something. It would be very quiet if they didn't.

The main team news was that one of the lynchpins of Saturday's wondrous performance, Ian Woan, was not named on the team-sheet. Sam Aiston was recalled and Gregor Rioch was back on the bench. There seemed to be some mystery surrounding this at the time but it turned out to be a case of protecting a slightly injured Woan by not playing him in one game rather than losing him from several.

As it turned out his omission was probably crucial. Town huffed and puffed almost as much as the winds, but never looked to recapture Saturday's form. They went behind early to a freakish own goal from Mick Heathcote. Rather than stirring them to heroic deeds, this knocked the stuffing out of them somewhat. Sam Aiston looked sharp once or twice but gradually faded from the game. Ryan Lowe worked hard and gained opportunities which he then squandered. Generally the team was ineffectual and the game was more and more run by Kidderminster's playing Dane, Bo Henrikson (their non-playing Dane being of course manager Jan Molby).

Kevin Ratcliffe was quite upbeat afterwards, saying he could not ask more of his boys in terms of effort. He might be right in that, but more than effort was required here tonight. To be fair, however, despite the disappointing result and the freezingly inhospitable winds, it was a game that held the attention. There were other moments of interest too, such as spotting Fred Davies wandering around at half-time, chatting to old acquaintances. There was also one nice moment when Kidderminster were about to take a corner at the end where I was sitting. The Shrewsbury subs were warming up in front of us and slightly obscuring the view. A couple of people in the crowd light-heartedly asked them to duck out of the way. As he complied, Peter Wilding cracked, "You don't want to see *them* score, do you?"

No coffee tonight, though I can recommend the renowned home-made Aggborough Soup – a little spicy for my taste, but welcome on such an evening.

On the subject of Fred Davies, I think I would say he was my least favourite Town manager. Yes, I know he was in charge when Town were promoted in 1994 and he is the only manager to take the town to Wembley, but he earns this title on two counts.

Firstly for his team selection at Wembley when he ignored loyal Town players and played loan players. He played John Kay at full back while Tommy Lynch sat on the bench and Kevin Seabury went only for the ride. He played Carl Robinson in midfield while Paul Evans missed out. Secondly for his treatment of a young man I will call John here, although it is not his real name. John was a pupil at the school where I teach. He was one of the most prodigiously talented schoolboy players I have seen and Salop signed him up. I saw the letter signed by Malcolm Starkey offering him a place when he finished school. I was delighted as this seemed good for both John and the Town. However, at the last minute Messrs Davies and Summerfield informed him that they were not going to take him on. He was stunned and I'm not sure whether he has really recovered now. I was ashamed that the football club that I had supported all my life was capable of such shoddy action.

Apart from John (who did play the odd game for the Salop youth team), the nearest I have come to teaching a footballer have been a cousin of Lee Chapman (formerly with several clubs including Stoke City, latterly more renowned as the husband of actress Lesley Ash), the daughter of a Villa ex-player and coach and a nephew of O'Neill "Tufty" Donaldson (Salop 1991-4). The brother of Michael Ricketts (Walsall and Bolton Wanderers) attended my school but I never taught him. I have taught a couple of champion Irish-dancers who ended up in Riverdance (one taking over the lead from Michael Flatley); but, spectacular as Irish-dancing is, it is not football. I did teach Simon Webbe who was in the same year as John and might himself have made it as a professional footballer but chose instead the relative sanity and security of a career in pop music as a singer with the band Blue. But enough of the frustrations of my time as a teacher.

Failure at Kidderminster was followed closely by the same at Rochdale. Although reports are that the performance merited better than the result, as with Kidderminster the bottom line is that we have no points whilst a promotion rival has three. The next two home games therefore gained in importance if we were to maintain any sort of challenge. The win against Swansea City was not only welcome in itself but vital as the others in the chase also picked up maximum points. Tony Lormor scored another, so that despite looking rusty and ineffectual he is at least producing some goals. The other two came from Ryan Lowe who was perhaps reacting to having been dropped to the subs' bench. There will now be something of a selection dilemma facing Mr Ratcliffe when Luke Rodgers becomes available against Halifax on Saturday.

All-time Salop Favourites Number Ten – Tony Kelly
"And Arsenal now have plenty of time to dictate the last few seconds." – Peter Jones

Tony Kelly was one of Salop's flawed geniuses. If the rest of his faculties could have complemented his football brain and his wider gifts have matched his footballing talents (and I don't just mean he needed to lose a bit of weight), he would have played in midfield for the Earth – or at least have been capped for England.

He was born in Prescot in October 1964, was an apprentice on Liverpool's books, had played for Wigan Athletic (98 League appearances), Stoke City (33 League appearances) and West Bromwich Albion (26 League appearances), as well as turning out for the humbler Prescot Cables and serving loan spells at Chester (5 League appearances) and Colchester (13 League appearances) before he joined Salop in February 1989. He played a hundred League games for us, in which he scored 15 goals – a reasonable return considering that he tended primarily to discharge a defensive role. He also played 15 FA Cup games (1 goal) and 8 League Cup games (1 goal) whilst at Salop.

At Salop he was a one-man team, a dynamo that unfortunately didn't always connect well with dimmer (in a footballing sense) team-mates, the foundation-stone on which rested a less than brilliant side. Shouldering such responsibility and work-load seemed to cause him some understandable frustration and annoyance with his less gifted colleagues at times and eventually probably led to him walking away from Salop (in the company of Mickey Brown) just before the 1991-2 season for an easier and more remunerative time at Bolton.

He put in 103 League appearances at Bolton before commencing a succession of brief sojourns at Port Vale, Millwall, Wigan, Peterborough and Altrincham, all on free transfers. This gipsy-like wandering from club to club throughout his career tells its own story. Four clubs had paid what were at the time reasonable fees for his services. In that respect Salop did the best out of him, acquiring him for the cut-price rate of £30,000 and receiving £100,000 when he left. That increase in his perceived value possibly reflects on the way that Salop had resurrected what appeared to be a failing talent.

I have two videos in which Tony Kelly not only plays an important part but also reveals that he was human. One is of the Arsenal game at the Gay Meadow in February 1991, when he was generally magnificent but a rare stray pass from him led to the goal, the ball being hoofed out of the Arsenal half for Kevin Campbell to latch onto and score.

The other video is one that I acquired by mistake. I had ordered the video of a decent League game played at Fellows Park in October 1989. Instead I was given one of a tedious preliminary round Leyland Daft Cup game played six weeks later. The video shows what is in many ways a typical Tony Kelly performance for Salop. He was playing sweeper and doing so with great vision and command. He was picking up any potential danger, making great interceptions and tackles, spraying long passes forward to Mickey Brown and Carl

Griffiths, taking all the free kicks, and occasionally surging forward. In the words of the commentator's understatement: "Kelly seems to be the outstanding player on the field tonight." However, there were a couple of incidents that underlined the problematic nature of his role and the reliance upon him that the team developed. On two occasions whilst attempting to play football he lost the ball on the wing just outside the penalty area; unlike the case of his Arsenal slip, on both of these occasions his blushes were spared by Walsall forwards missing open goals.

Saturday 9th March, 2002

"If you can't stand the heat in the dressing-room, get out of the kitchen." – Terry Venables

Halifax Town (home); Football League Division Three

Previous record in league games:					
Home			Away		
Win	Draw	Lose	Win	Draw	Lose
7	7	1	4	6	6

3-0 (HT 1-0); Heathcote (1), Rodgers (55), Aiston (74)
Attendance: 3,729
Standpoint: Once more on the Riverside against a second tier barrier near the penalty area at the Station End.

Fears of flooding are in temporary abeyance; the silted up patch of land that climbs out of the Severn up to the bank beside the English Bridge looks like a beach that the tide has recently left. Umbrellas are being inverted all over town; blizzards stalk the North of these islands; Hereford's game has been called off because of fears over the stadium's safety in the winds; corrugated sheets will be torn from the roof of the St Andrews stand and sent spinning like razor-edged Frisbees, luckily only to plough into empty seats. Strangely enough, however, this afternoon's game at Gay Meadow did not seem to be too affected by the wind.

The Halifax fans look to have given up the cause. Their team is well adrift now and looking a good bet to drop out of the League for a second time. There are only a handful standing at the Station End and virtually none in the Visitors' seating section. The stay-away fans may not have grasped the fact that this could be the last time these two Clubs will meet one another. Their mascot nevertheless remains in good spirits; before the game he is giving out sweets to the Salop fans and even joins in with the Uptown Girls.

The presence is announced of several primary schools, including Prees where I started my school life almost fifty years ago. At 2.57 a steam train chugs out of the station. The scene is set.

It was never going to be pretty and for the most part it wasn't. It was too one-sided to be great football. The goals were nicely worked and there were some near misses but it was a game where the win mattered more than the manner of its achieving.

Today's sugar packet featured Dr Roger Bannister, the first man to run the four-minute mile. Salop didn't need even that long. Within a minute Sam Aiston was fouled to the right of the penalty area. Ian Woan chipped the ball over to the far post where Heathcote headed in. After that it looked like a question of how many, but unfortunately it was domination without penetration. At times it resembled a playground game of shooting-in. Aiston hit the bar, Murray had a shot well saved, there were goal-line clearances.

In the midst of this Luke Rodgers was having a private battle to get back into things. Kevin Ratcliffe had gone for the logical solution of bringing him in to play alongside target-man Lormor, which meant that two-goal Ryan Lowe was unfortunately on the bench. It was a combination that seemed to have promise and led directly to the second goal when Lormor (greatly improved since his rusty debut) put Rodgers through for a free run. This was Luke's reward for his keenness and bustle.

Earlier in the game, however, his anxiety to do well had got him booked. He committed a silly foul after a mere ten minutes back from his enforced mid-season break. His over-eagerness was mainly to blame but I think bad refereeing also shared in the responsibility. If a referee permits the speedier and more skilful players such as Luke or Sam to be pushed, pulled, elbowed, tripped, kicked, etc, he should recognise that players who have to put up with such treatment deserve some leniency when they reciprocate the aggression. There may also have been an element of a macho referee reaction to Luke Rodgers's unfortunate reputation. There was certainly inconsistency in that worse fouls by other players later went unpunished, whilst Karl Murray was booked because of the reaction of the Halifax player rather than the foul he had committed. I was also mystified at one point as to why a free-kick was awarded against Matt Redmile when he had played the ball a good yard before his opponent arrived.

The third Salop goal came via route one. Halifax had gained a corner from a strange backward clearance by Karl Murray, but Dunbavin claimed the ball and kicked upfield. Sam Aiston and Luke Rodgers both raced through, and with the latter creating a diversion the former controlled the ball and coolly lobbed it over the keeper for one of his best ever finishes.

In the last ten minutes or so the Riverside youth were so under-thrilled that, after having exhausted the celebration of each member of the Salop team, they resorted to crude chants and the taunting of Halifax fans. The most disturbing aspect to this was that the designated fat-man and slapper responded in a far from seemly fashion. When you've travelled all that way to watch your team sink deeper in the relegation mire, the last thing you need is to lose your dignity into the bargain.

The Ages of Fan – Number Two: The Youth

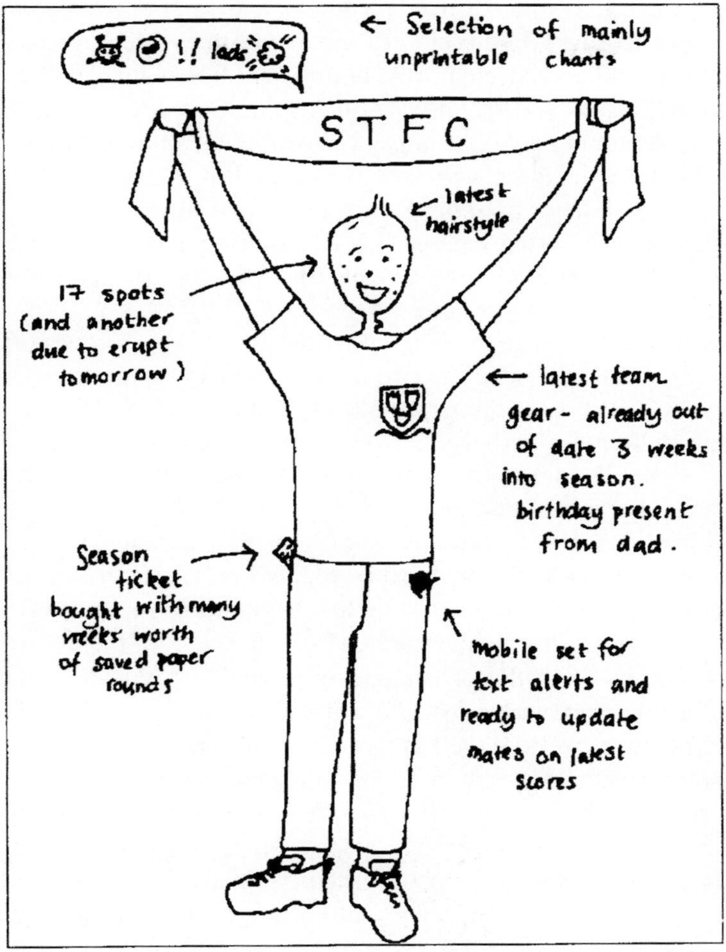

Interesting Times

"Many clubs have a question mark in the shape of an axe-head hanging over them." – Malcolm McDonald

A week after the Halifax demolition Salop were returning to the scene of the Great Escape at St James's, Exeter. Thanks to goals from Luke ("I can head the ball too") Rodgers and Matt ("What's the big deal about scoring?") Redmile, we achieved a draw, although many at the club would consider that two points lost. It was not immediately critical because of the way other results went. One or two other teams seem to be running out of steam at a critical point. Hull and Mansfield appear to have the jitters and to be forgetting how to win. Cheltenham have games in hand but may be too exhausted to make them count. Football is such a funny game that the Halifax team that looked so washed out at the Meadow suddenly start fighting for their life and defeat both Kidderminster and Cheltenham.

Salop's season may actually boil down to how we perform at Rushden and Diamonds. The two teams are currently neck and neck, so a victor in this encounter would gain more than a psychological advantage. Matters on the team front are, however, far from simple for Town. Andy Thompson has gone back to Cardiff after his loan spell but has now been released by the Welsh club so there is the possibility that Town may now sign him on a permanent basis. Of more significance is the recall to Hartlepool of Tony Lormor. After a sluggish and unimpressive start he had begun to show signs of being what was needed as complement to Luke Rodgers in the absence of Nigel Jemson. He had scored a couple of goals, provided one or two useful feeds, and was proving a valuable loan signing. Hartlepool have obviously realised their error in allowing him to come to a club that was a rival for a promotion play-off spot. Unfortunately for them their realisation was only after they had apparently dropped out of contention whilst the player had helped Town to stay in the running. Kevin Ratcliffe, having been spurned by Wolves' Shropshire-born Adam Proudlock, is now looking at players such as Brett Angell of Walsall. Incidentally KR has himself signed a new three year contract, which repays the Board's faith in giving him the last one at the point when things were looking particularly black a couple of years ago.

In Europe Manchester United and Liverpool have progressed in style to the quarter finals of the UEFA Champions League. On the other hand Arsenal put up a tepid performance against a Juventus reserve team and lost out to small town German side Bayer Leverkusen and the euphonious Portuguese Deportivo La Coruna.

The week has also contained the saga of the game between Sheffield United and West Bromwich Albion (A.K.A. the Battle of Bramall Lane), which had to be abandoned because Sheffield lacked the minimum number of players for the match to continue, following three sendings-off, two players withdrawn through alleged injury, and all substitutes having been used. For a change, the referee was absolutely correct in his decisions. He had no choice concerning any of the three dismissals, the last two being despicable acts of thuggery. It was good to see that Steve Jagielka's little brother Phil was behaving sensibly amidst the mayhem. It is to Sheffield United's credit that they have at least sacked the two perpetrators of violent conduct, although there is still a question mark over other things that may have been going on. West Brom have been awarded the three points for the game – any other outcome would have set a dangerous precedent. Let's just hope that their final League position does not depend on goal difference.

Possibly of even greater importance to the survival of the beautiful game in this country has been the ITV Digital affair. Essentially ITV Digital has miscalculated the appeal of televised League football to the extent that it is now insisting that the deal it made with the Football League must be renegotiated. The Football League is naturally not keen on that idea, as clubs have budgeted for, or even already spent, the money due to them under the original agreement. As ever filthy lucre is at the bottom of it all. The two wealthy television companies that own ITV Digital are not rushing to rescue their prodigal offspring. There are dire prophecies that half the clubs in the Football League could go out of business if this goes belly-up, and even that the whole house of cards could collapse, Premiership too – and all because someone did not grasp that not only was there already sufficient televised football but that the appeal of League football is being there rather than watching a televised version. I would watch Salop on television if the opportunity arose but have no desire to watch other Second and Third Division games on a regular basis. Maybe football's salvation lies in the moves to cap players' wages. Some sanity has to be brought to a world where Premiership players are demanding salaries that would keep an average League club afloat for the season.

A more light-hearted football-related story concerns a study of how tuneful the singing is at the Premiership grounds. Apparently the most harmonious choir belongs to Southampton. I don't know whether they tried comparing like with like or even took into account the differing technical demands of songs associated with particular clubs. Likewise I don't know where Town's fans would come in such a league table – they'd probably class as enthusiastic and boisterous rather than melodic and sweetly synchronised.

Rushden and Diamonds 3 Shrewsbury Town 0

Oops…

That means we have slipped out of the top seven, we have joined the band of ditherers and our fate is no longer in our own hands. The newspaper account said we were the stronger team in the second half and I heard Kevin Ratcliffe reported as saying that apart from the three goals it was an even contest. So that's OK then, Kevin – what do the odd three goals matter?

Let's be positive. We need to look for maximum points from the last five games. Three are at home. Four are against teams with nothing to play for. On paper the only tough one should be the final game against Luton, and perhaps by then they will already have their position decided and not be over-competitive. Some of our fellow contenders have to face each other and thus scrap over the same points. Let's be positive.

Transfer deadline passes very quietly this year – few clubs prepared to blow the millions they don't actually possess, for some reason. Salop have made two signings: Andy Thompson, as expected, and Steve Guinan, to plug the current big-man-up-front vacancy.

Saturday 30th March, 2002

"I'm a firm believer that if the other side scores first you have to score twice to win." – Howard Wilkinson

Torquay United (home); Football League Division Three

Previous record in league games:					
Home			Away		
Win	Draw	Lose	Win	Draw	Lose
14	5	5	5	4	16

0-1 (HT 0-1)
Attendance: 4,510
Standpoint: Yet again on the Riverside, against a second tier barrier in line with the edge of the penalty area at the Station End.

The games was preceded by an impeccably observed silence for Town's former chairman, Tim Yates, who died during the week.

At 3.03 Torquay scored.

At 3.15 the Queen Mother died.

Easter Eggs

"You must be as strong in March, when the fish are down." – Gianluca Vialli

The best that can be said about Saturday's game is that it will not live long in the memory, or at least one hopes it won't. Having written "oops" after the Rushden result I was tempted to "whoops" this time. As Greavesie used to say, "It's a funny old game". That Town can do the double over Plymouth Argyle and have the same done to them by Torquay United is the sort of mystery that maintains interest in football and prevents everyone from winning the pools.

There did not look to be the massive gap between the two teams that the League table suggests. Indeed in the person of Marcus Richardson Torquay had the most dangerous looking player on the pitch (though ironically the goal he scored was a toe-poke from one yard that most Subuteo players could have managed). Were the Town players showing the tiredness of a long season? Was the pressure getting to them, as it is obviously getting to Mansfield and Hull (both of whom slipped up again)? Is Luke Rodgers losing confidence (earlier in the season he would not have had the ball taken off his toes by a keeper as he rounded him on his way to goal)? Was it a collective off-day?

One gent behind me in the crowd believed he knew the answer. It was essentially down to the fact that Kevin Ratcliffe hasn't got a clue about football, just doesn't know what he's doing. That, I presume, is the Kevin Ratcliffe who played at the top level in this country, who captained his country on numerous occasions, who has steadily improved the League position of Salop over the last three seasons?

The programme mentioned a "Player behind the ball competition" that had been in the Mansfield programme. Based on the number on the shorts (beginning with "2"), the length of sleeve (short) and the make of boot (Adidas), I had reckoned it had to be Tony Lormor. The answer given in the Halifax programme had consequently amazed me because it was stated to be Ian Woan (who does not wear Adidas boots). In the Torquay programme they weren't exactly admitting they'd got it wrong, but in response to a couple of complaints that had been accompanied with reasons they were awarding another prize.

This leads me on to making a disclaimer of my own. I have tried throughout to be accurate about facts, but sometimes they are slippery little things. For example, the statistics given in programmes concerning the past meetings between clubs do not always tally. Then there is the matter of Arthur Rowley's record – was it 433 or 434? Different sources give different figures. In many ways writing fiction is much easier – you just make up your own "facts". I have, as I said, made an honest effort to get my statistics correct, to distinguish between Wayne and Brian Williams, not to refer to Simon Shakeshaft as "Steve", and so on (though I admit to a certain amount of confusion in differentiating between Fred Davies, former Coracle Man, and Fred Davies, former Manager), but I would not wish anyone to lose money betting on the complete accuracy of what I have written.

After Easter Monday we are still in with a chance of the play-offs. A last minute goal from Jamie Tolley gave Salop the victory over Lincoln City, after Luke Rodgers's early goal had been cancelled out. Matters are no longer in our own hands, but if (and that is a big IF) we win the three remaining fixtures and others make a slip-up or two, anything is possible. It would be great to win the next two games and finish the League programme needing to beat already-promoted Luton at the Meadow.

The Blue-and-Amber web-site perpetrated a rather nice April Fool – the only one I came across this year. The basic theme was that Salop were to sign young Arsenal star Jermaine Pennant on loan for the whole of next season (so that he could improve his game). – We wish! And that is precisely the point. The beauty of the best hoax stories is that not only are they are credible, but they also play on the audience's desire that they should be true.

More bad news for the Football League. Just as they are gearing themselves up for a fight with ITV Digital and its parents, they are hit by the withdrawal of sponsorship for the league cup by Worthington. Oh well: it never rains but it pours. People who live in glasshouses should not site them next to football pitches. It's a long game that has no whistle. Many hands make goalkeeping easy. Every crowd has a copper watching. Too many crooks spoil the Board. One man's Home is another man's Away.

All-time Salop Favourites Number Eleven – Tommy Lynch

"The one thing England have got is spirit, resolve, grit and determination." – Alan Hansen

Tommy Lynch was a whole-hearted, solid and uncompromising full-back who gave his all for the team. As a result the crowd loved him and he in turn fed off their encouragement. This was encapsulated in his delayed appearance at Wembley. It is one of Fred Davies's greatest tactical errors not to have played Tommy from the start or at least to have realised the need to unleash him sooner. When Tommy eventually entered the arena Town at last played with some passion and it was he who initiated the move that set up Mark Taylor to score our consolation goal. Unfortunately it was all too late.

Tommy Lynch was born in Limerick in October 1964 and played for his home town team before moving across the water to join Sunderland in 1988. He was with Sunderland for a year and a half but failed to establish himself there, playing only four League games. In January 1990 he joined Salop for £20,000. In a little over six years he played 220 League games (plus 14 as sub) in which he scored 14 goals, several from the penalty spot. These were generally thunderbolts, for a ball struck by Tommy knew that it had been truly walloped. He also played some 46 other assorted games (FA Cup, League Cup, etc.) in which he managed another couple of goals. After leaving us he returned to Ireland and has had stints managing Waterford (a Waterford web-site says: "Tommy Lynch's first season as player/manager had built a solid foundation for a successful 1998 season when promotion as champions was finally achieved") and Limerick.

With his mass of red hair and stocky build, Tommy somehow contrived to look smaller than his actual six-foot. He was one of the hardest tacklers to have trodden the Meadow and made the left-back slot his own for a long time. He was, however, more versatile than that and played occasional games in such exotic positions as centre-half, midfield and centre-forward.

A limerick for the boy from Limerick:

There was a full-back called Lynch
Whose tackles might make you flinch.
His headers strong;
His clearances long;
He never yielded an inch.

The Tommy Interview
"His tackle was definitely pre-ordained." – Glenn Hoddle

My thanks to Tom for his generosity with his time. His feelings for the Town are evident in the following interview. In addition he referred in an e-mail to "all the fine players who have donned our proud jersey" and mentioned "many fine and happy times we (my better half Christine and I) enjoyed both on and off the pitch." Those who saw him in action will probably not be surprised by his enthusiasm and genuineness.

ALAN: How did you become a professional footballer?

TOMMY: I played football for Limerick part-time and went to Gillingham on trial. I got a call from Denis Smith, saying did I want to sign for Sunderland (they needed a left sided player cheap). So I signed.

ALAN: What was the high-point of your footballing career?

TOMMY: The highpoint was walking off the pitch at the Meadow for the last time. Everyone knew I was going home and Fred Davies called me ashore a few minutes early. The reception I got coming off the pitch will stay with me forever.

ALAN: What sort of memories have you of your time at STFC? – Did you enjoy your time there?

TOMMY: Memories were all good, too many to mention but I loved my time at the Town. I got on well with all and basically had a ball.

ALAN: What are your memories of Salop's trip to Wembley?

TOMMY: Wembley was OK. I was gutted I didn't play from the start. I should have led out the team as I was captain, but what hurt most was Fred called Steve Anthrobus aside and explained to him his reasons for not playing. I was told in front of everyone I was not playing. I was the longest serving player, but not given that courtesy.

ALAN: What other matches do you particularly remember?

TOMMY: Other matches were the semi away to Bristol Rovers – we were going to Wembley which was a dream come true; the year we won the league the matches at home to Preston and Hereford; the Blackburn, Wimbledon and Arsenal games.

ALAN: Who did you most enjoy playing alongside?

TOMMY: I enjoyed playing alongside Carl Griffiths ["Pinhead"] – funny lad, easy to get going.

ALAN: Were there any particular opponents you particularly enjoyed playing against?

TOMMY: I loved playing against Mickey Brown when he was at Bolton – used to put the fear of god up him.

ALAN: Who in the game did you most respect?

TOMMY: Kevin Summerfield – a solid pro, family man, nice fella.

ALAN: Who were the particular characters in the game in your day (apart from yourself, of course)?

TOMMY: Characters? – easy… Chris Withe and Mark "Foxy" Hughes, the funniest blokes ever.

ALAN: Did you have any particular superstitions or special pre-match routines?

TOMMY: I had a couple of superstitions. I wore the same suit and travelled to the pitch the same way. I was an antichrist to live with on matchdays.

ALAN: Do you have any regrets about your career? — Would you change anything?

TOMMY: I should and could have tried much harder at Sunderland.

ALAN: Was there anything about football as a career that you didn't like?

TOMMY: I didn't like travel at Christmas, leaving Christine alone. Other than that I was well looked after. – I hated losing!

ALAN: What was particularly hard about being a professional footballer?

TOMMY: There was nothing hard at all being a pro. We were blessed, the chosen few.

ALAN: Which manager did you most enjoy working with?

TOMMY: I enjoyed working with Fred, although we had our moments. I shall never forget when Molly was born. The team was due to go to Fulham in the Cup. Fred told me he wasn't taking me – family was most important. Asa Hartford was great, but I didn't get to work with him long enough. Bondy just wasn't my type as a person but we got on OK.

ALAN: Did you feel in any way special or lucky to be a footballer?

TOMMY: I loved being a footballer, waking up, going to work knowing it's going to be a great day. Lucky I was blessed.

ALAN: Was it difficult making the transition from football to your life-after-football?

TOMMY: I had no difficulty making the transition. After my time at Shrewsbury I managed Waterford and Limerick. I eased my way out of full-time football.

ALAN: How did your family handle your being a footballer?

TOMMY: Christine found it tough at times, my being away from home for Christmas. I missed my brother's and sisters' weddings, birthdays etc., but still I feel it was a small price to pay.

ALAN: Would you encourage your son to become a professional footballer?

TOMMY: My son Jack is four and kicks a ball day and night. As long as he is happy doing what he wants it's OK by me. I wouldn't be one for shoving a golf club or racket or cue in his hand, telling him to practise.

ALAN: Have you retained any links with the club?

TOMMY: I still follow the fortunes of the Town. Any time I'm in Shrewsbury I call into the club. At the end of the day I had seven great years, it was my home, my girl was born there. I will always have a place in my heart for the club and the town and the people of Shrewsbury who made our time there an experience we wouldn't change for love nor money.

The Ages of Fan – Number Three: The Mature Man

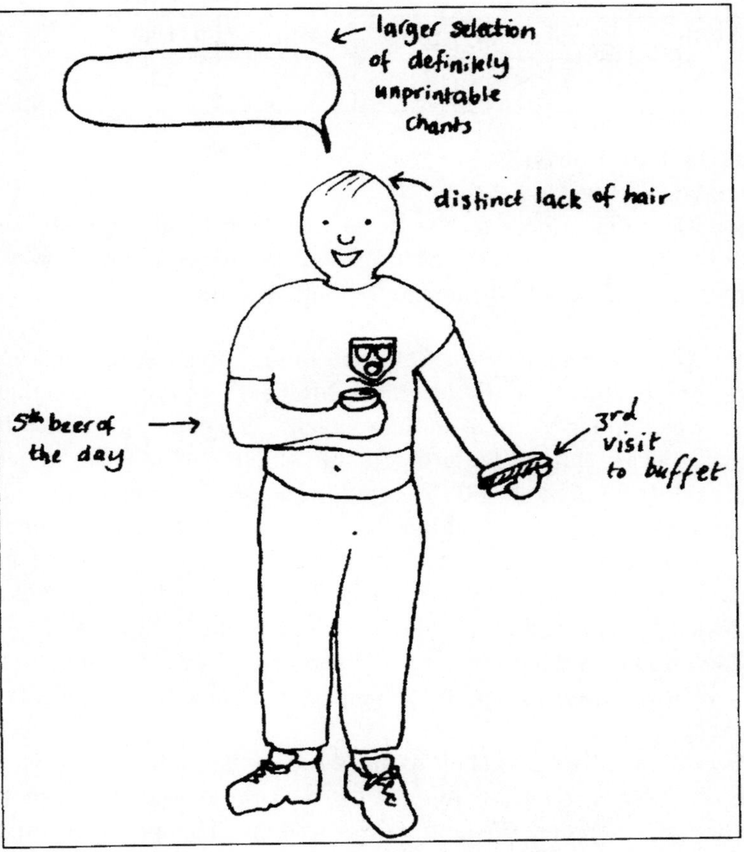

Saturday 6th April, 2002
"We had enough chances to win this game. In fact, we did win." – Alex Smith

Carlisle United (home); Football League Division Three

Previous record in league games:					
Home			Away		
Win	Draw	Lose	Win	Draw	Lose
5	7	4	3	5	9

1-0 (HT 1-0); Lowe (39)
Attendance: 3,969
Standpoint: Once more on the Riverside against a second tier barrier near the penalty area at the Station End; in the second half on a first tier barrier fractionally nearer to the half-way line.

I was hoping that the second one-minute silence in consecutive home games (this time for the Queen Mother) would not mean that the spirit was drained away from Salop again. The game turned out to be a tense affair but at least the team adopted a positive attacking approach from the kick-off. We could (and maybe should) have been several goals in the lead within the first five minutes. This somehow set the pattern for the game. Town were always on top but never converted that supremacy into goals. The only goal was a cracker: a free kick taken by Mick Heathcote from about the half-way line was nodded down by Matthew Redmile and Ryan Lowe hit a thunderbolt of a volley from the edge of the penalty area that gave the keeper no chance.

By then Carlisle had been reduced to ten men when Peter Murphy was sent off in the 21st minute for the sort of nasty and reckless tackle that often doesn't even gain a booking. This proved ultimately to be no help to Salop in scoring goals. They had periods when they passed the ball from one to another like Brazil might, but without achieving the telling final pass. However, creating chances was not the problem. There were chances aplenty. Several players could have had hat-tricks, including Steve Guinan who apart from failing to score had a useful game bustling and harrying. There were several brilliant saves by Peter Keen, the Carlisle keeper; goal-line clearances; shots that struck the post; centres that no-one managed to make contact with; shots that missed the target by the width of a coat of paint; shots that missed the target by a whole gallery of paintings.

This was all part of that special end of season feeling, a cocktail of excitement, frustration, adrenalin, fear, hope, agony. That Town had only a one goal lead and Carlisle (particularly in the shape of Richie Foran) had the potential to score if given the slightest opportunity maintained the tension to the end. That Carlisle did not equalise in the dying moments (Foran did head over the bar) is an indicator of Town's improved fortunes this season. I have been to so many games over the years which Town have dominated only to be denied a win or even defeated through a late goal.

For the last few minutes of the game Luke Rodgers was quite rightly withdrawn. He had been venting his frustrations with some niggly challenges and had just been booked. He was obviously displeased at being substituted and made as though to storm off down the tunnel – only to be diverted onto the bench by a near rugby tackle from Assistant Manager Dave Fogg. Luke's aggression is an important asset and leads to many of his goals. He still needs, however, a higher level of maturity to be able to focus that aggression and also to appreciate that Kevin Ratcliffe can see a wider picture – to remove Luke from the game at that point meant that he would not be red-carded and missing more games.

We are still outside the play-off positions but it's not all over. At this stage nerves start to play an important part, adding to the usual delicious uncertainties of football – and that applies to all the teams involved. Gaining maximum points from Southend and Luton might not be easy, but no other match is going to be cut-and-dried either.

A post-script to the game is that Carlisle have sacked their manager, Roddy Collins (brother of boxer, Steve) – not because the team lost to Salop but because of comments he made about the future of his own club. This seems unfortunate for Carlisle in that he has pulled them up from what have been a few rocky years that have seen them flirting seriously with the Conference, including that memorable last gasp goal by on-loan goalkeeper Jimmy Glass and finishing above Chester on goal-difference the year that Salop escaped. It is a pity that some clubs are fated to be controlled by those whose football knowledge is less than their egos.

Some Light Relief

"I dreamt of playing for a club like Manchester United, and now here I am at Liverpool." – Sander Westerveld

Here is arguably one of the best football jokes. A minimal knowledge of Shakespeare is essential.

Is it true that the Liverpool coach used to play for Nottingham Forest and the Everton coach was with Notts County?

Yes. The quality of Mersey is Notts trained.

Entering the Final Straight

"As we say in football, it'll go down to the last wire." – Colin Todd

With a goal each for Ian Woan and Ryan Lowe, Salop have prevailed at Southend. In so doing we are back in the play-off positions (as Rushden and Scunthorpe both lost), and have surely also established a record for the number of points won by a team with less than eleven men. Sandwiched between the two goals was the sending-off of Luke Rodgers for "violent conduct"; Kevin Ratcliffe's preventative measure of withdrawing Luke before the end of last week's game looks to have been wasted. Ceefax reported that Salop were considering an appeal against the sending off. I wished I shared Kevin's optimism in the face of experience; the Club is prepared to risk £2,000 on the chance that a referee might admit he was wrong. Let us dwell on positive matters, however, and celebrate the team's achievement. It is a sign of their spirit that, whereas in recent years they would have folded as soon as adversity came on the scene, they now show this never-say-die attitude that pulls them together at such moments. The cry of "We only need ten men" would have echoed around Roots Hall.

The top of the table now looks like this:

		Home					Away						
	P	W	D	L	F	A	W	D	L	F	A	Gd	Pts
Plymouth	44	18	2	2	39	11	11	7	4	26	16	38	96
Luton	45	15	5	3	50	18	14	2	6	44	30	46	94
Cheltenham	44	11	11	1	40	20	10	3	8	26	27	19	77
Mansfield	45	16	3	3	47	24	7	4	12	23	36	10	76
Rochdale	45	12	8	2	39	21	8	7	8	24	30	12	75
Rushden	45	14	5	4	40	20	5	8	9	25	31	14	70
Shrewsbury	45	13	4	5	36	17	7	6	10	28	34	13	70
Hartlepool	45	12	6	5	53	23	7	5	10	19	25	24	68
Scunthorpe	45	13	5	4	42	22	5	9	9	31	34	17	68

The end-of-season shake-down is becoming a little clearer. Plymouth and Luton have been in a different class and are definitely promoted. Plymouth could actually achieve a century of points. The third automatic spot is between Cheltenham, Mansfield and Rochdale, though Cheltenham must be favourites being in front and having an extra game in hand. The competition for the last two play-off places is finely balanced. Rushden and Salop could take them if they hold their nerve and pick up the points from their last games, but Scunthorpe and Hartlepool (who have had a resurgence of late, culminating in a seven goal romp yesterday) are waiting for any slip up. Town have put themselves in charge again. Now we have merely to beat Luton next weekend….

Let's look at that a little more closely. Luton, with Plymouth, have stood out from the rest of the teams in the Third Division this season. Historically Town have encountered Luton on relatively few occasions because Luton have generally lived in more exalted company. They have also tended to get the better of us, beating us at the Meadow more times than we have prevailed and allowing us only one away victory (though that was 7-2, in March 1965). The portents are therefore not favourable. This is, however, football and not only will we be highly charged and highly motivated but we can at least reassure ourselves with the knowledge that we have done the double over Plymouth.

I see that a poll of Rochdale fans indicated that their overwhelming preference for play-off opponents would be Shrewsbury Town. This is somewhat double-edged as it shows they think we would be the easiest opposition but also supposes that we would have qualified.

I take back all that I have said about referees (well, some). Mr Richards has overturned his decision about red-carding Luke Rodgers. This makes Luke available should we progress as far as the play-offs. There is even word that Nigel Jemson might be ready for a come-back.

Saturday 20th April, 2002
"It's the end of season curtain raiser." – Peter Withe

Luton Town (home); Football League Division Three

Previous record in league games:					
Home			Away		
Win	Draw	Lose	Win	Draw	Lose
3	1	4	1	3	5

0-2 (HT 0-1)
Attendance: 7,858; all ticket [mine was 00258]
Standpoint: On the Riverside, against a front-line barrier between the half-way line and the penalty area at the Station End.

The daffodils (remnants of the "Britain in Bloom" competition from a few years ago) are fading on the grassy slope beneath the former Royal Shropshire Infirmary. The swans are nesting below the English Bridge; let's hope they have better luck with the floods this year. The birds are singing fit to bust and for that matter the grass is anything but withered from the sedge. Furthermore I shall be home in daylight. These are all signs of spring's advance and the consequent end of the English football season, although of course, with the play-offs and it being a World Cup year, football is far from finished yet. It is, however, for Salop.

On the day it was a match too far against the one team in the Division that was capable of easily holding Salop. Luton were professional if not exciting and should do well next season in the higher sphere. Today they were content to sit back and soak up the pressure that Salop exerted and hit us on the break. They rarely looked in any trouble and, despite playing much of the game in their half, were the team that had most clear goal chances. The last minute goal might have been cruel to Salop but Luton had already missed several straightforward openings.

The build-up to the game had been excellent and the fans had responded well to provide a terrific atmosphere in the ground. There was plenty of blue-and-amber – some young lads in front of me even resembled mutant badgers with a blue stripe down their yellow dyed hair. The Luton fans were also colourful and many wore their trademark hats. Unfortunately the Luton team hadn't given much credence to the hype that it would be a fairy-tale Shrewsbury victory.

Most memorable crowd comment of the day was one addressed to a diminutive assistant referee: "Get back to Snow White!" This was prompted by the official making an adjudication with which someone in the crowd apparently disagreed. I must say that generally speaking the officials ran the game quite well.

There were three attempts to cash in on the emotion of the occasion and the high turnout of fans. The first was by a political party that I won't name (both in the interests of maintaining political balance and not to encourage them) whose supporters distributed leaflets purporting to support the New Meadow but which seemed to me to represent a rather transparent attempt to canvass votes for the forthcoming local elections.

The second piece of self-promotion was by the Shropshire Star, who were distributing free copies of a special issue. If they wish to promote their paper in this way, that's fine by me. A newspaper with pictures of Salop in action is worth all the broken promises of politicians.

The third case was that of a gentleman who emerged from the crowd a little to my right and streaked to the centre circle and back. He had nothing on apart from some writing that decorated several of his body surfaces. As he was led away (now with trousers on) it was possible to see that the writing (which I hope had not been done with a permanent marker) mentioned a local company. This incident lightened the atmosphere but was not well-timed, coming in the last few minutes of the game when the footballers needed their last dregs of concentration. He could have offered his exhibitionism as a contribution to the half-time entertainment or have had the sense to wait for the final whistle – though maybe the police cordon would have rendered such a manoeuvre difficult at that point.

Talking of this police cordon, one aspect of the afternoon that I particularly regret is the heavy-handed insistence that no-one should come onto the pitch at the end of the game. It seems that we are so frightened of trouble these days that we eliminate much of the potentially joyful. I can remember last-games-of-the-season in the past when we would all be on the pitch after the final whistle. There was nothing sinister, nasty, dangerous or health-threatening about this. It was a celebration, a chance to tread the hallowed turf. As recently as the promotion year of 1994 we still managed this at the Meadow and the pitch at Exeter was harmlessly swamped only a couple of years back. – And was there any aggro? Was anyone injured? Was the pitch or its fittings damaged? Was anyone intent on anything other than having a good time.

There have been ugly scenes at the end of the season (– and there was apparently trouble on Saturday in the Wakeman stand, though that is a different issue). The match against Middlesbrough in 1986 springs to mind. There have also been instances of the merely annoying, such as when West Bromwich Albion, like unwelcome guests at a party, hi-jacked Salop's wake in 1992 by insisting on holding their own celebrations on the Meadow pitch.

However, it should be possible to read the mood of the occasion a little better and be flexible enough that the crowd can be treated as humans, not as hooligans or cattle. The chant of "What a waste of money" as the entire West Mercia constabulary appeared just before the final whistle was a fair comment. The wages of these gentlemen (who were actually carrying a separate riot helmet as well as wearing an ordinary one), together with the cost of their dogs and their petrol, to say nothing of the helicopter that spent several hours in the area, must have been phenomenal. I can recall thirty odd years ago when what stewards there were kept a low profile and the police presence wasn't much more than my old school-mate Chris Mellor. Are we that much more uncivilised now?

Both of my sugar sachets contained the image of Big Ben, possibly a double reminder that the time was up for Salop, the chimes have rung out the season. Send not to know for whom the bells tolls….

On the way home, to the injury of watching Salop fail was added the insult of being stuck in a line of cars for many minutes whilst first a policeman waved through traffic heading for Luton and then the lights were set to an apparently permanent red. They might still be stuck on red for all I know; after an impatient wait I extricated myself from the queue and sought an alternative route.

The Ages of Fan – Number Four: Old Age and Wisdom

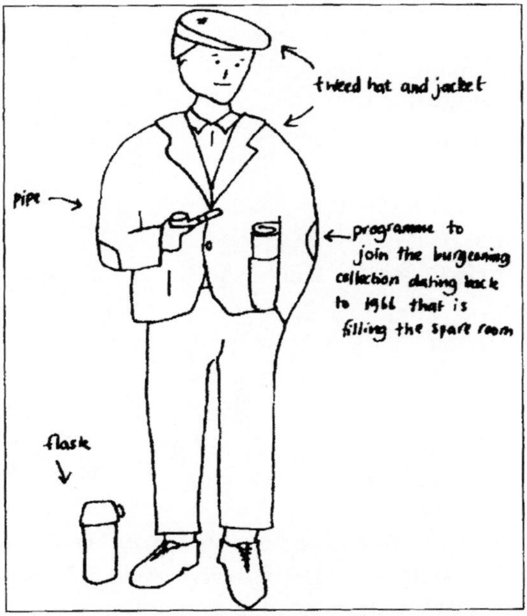

N.B. It is imperative that the tweed cap be removed whilst the owner is driving – otherwise speed is reduced by at least 20 m.p.h. and reactions become erratic.

Poetic Interlude Four — Football 1985
"We rose both at an instant, and fought a long hour by Shrewsbury clock." – (W.Shakespeare, Henry IV, Part 1: V.iv.148)

P.O.W. camps and football stadia
both have floodlights
and barbed-wire perimeters.
Football has always been war;
an enemy's severed head
the ball.
The fans' singing is a tribal chant,
a battle-cry.

If, for forty years,
pretending we are now civilised
we starve Britain's youth
of European blood,
deny them their manhood rite –
if they are not allowed
to kill with bullet and bomb
what do we expect?

At Loggerheads
"It is better to marry a shrew than a sheep." – 16th century proverb.

The original version of the following appeared in *A Large Scotch*, Issue 9:

A CHANGE IN LOGO?

With regard to the question of the Club's logo, I would like to make a few personal observations. Football is very much an affair of the heart; attachment to a particular club is emotional not rational. Why else would I still be supporting Shrewsbury Town after living in Birmingham for the past twenty-five years? My emotional reaction to the advent of the shrew logo was roughly as follows:

1. **Irritation and annoyance** that the club I had been cheering on for years under the various soubriquets of "you blues", "the Town" or "Salop" was suddenly referred to in the media as "the Shrews", it being implied that this was what fans called, and always had called, the Club. I still cannot recall any general acceptance of the term on the Riverside or anywhere else within the ground (although, never having frequented it, I cannot answer for the Directors' box). It is an ad-man's invention.

2. **Bewilderment** at the choice of logo. I think the actual design is rather cute, but what image of the club is it supposed to portray? How, one wonders, are the Shrews likely to fare against, for example, Owls, Wolves or Gunners? The old loggerheads was not only a tougher image, but also one that reflected the fact that Shrewsbury Town Football Club is more than Shrewsbury's team, it represents Shropshire. If it were desirable to have inflatables, cuddly toys, etc. to promote the image of the club, why not use one of the big cats from the loggerheads? Just because "Shrew" is the first syllable of Shrewsbury does not mean it is either necessary or desirable to use it for the club's logo. The practice of punning on the name might work for Wolverhampton and Swansea, but it is not universally a good idea. It would probably not be welcomed by Wrexham, Scarborough or Chester. Wigan would be the Wigs, Kidderminster the Kids and a certain team from North London would be the butt of a lot of jokes. In short, most clubs would be advised to avoid this trend like Gazza the attentions of Vinny Jones. Still it could have been worse: it might have been decided that the Town's logo should be a sharp-tongued woman.

3. **Alienation** at not being consulted about the change. The important questions behind this issue are: "Why was the change necessary?" and "Who should make a decision?" The first of these is open to debate, but was it ever debated (other than at Board or Promotions Officer level)? My answer to the second question is implicit in all that I have

written so far: such a decision should not be made without the blessing of those with the greatest long-term interest in the Club – the fans.

Since I wrote this it is probably true that Salop are more frequently referred to as the Shrews. There has been what one might call a creeping acceptance. If I'm honest I don't care so much. I even have a Salop mug with a shrew on it. Things change.

It is interesting that my suggestion about possibly using "one of the big cats from the loggerheads" prefigured Lennie the Lion.

Frank exercises his right of reply
or
They also serve who do not stand and shout
or
Far from the madding crowd, but very interested in the result
or
Forever Amber & Blue
or
The Town & I
or
Following Shrewsbury — at a safe distance

"It's a bitter pill to swallow, but we have to take it on the chin. " – Terry Neil, sometime Manager of Arsenal.

You can choose the sort of music you listen to, or the colour of your socks. You can choose the work you do, or the person you marry. You cannot choose your parents, where you are born, or the football club you support. For better or worse you're stuck with all of these.

So you begin your life in Prees, a quite ordinary little affair in North Shropshire, which will not benefit from a bypass for some years yet. The house is on Shrewsbury Street, and that's the town to which you'll soon discover all roads lead, literally and metaphorically: route centre and heart of whatever spirit proud Salopians can muster. Salop the town, Salop the county.

After the first momentous move of my life (a few miles further into Shropshire) I attended Ellerdine County Primary. The building now, I believe, is a house with a double garage, but there I learnt we lived in the largest inland county. Think of that! Something we're best at. Yet in no time you discover there's nothing there, only fields and a few houses between them – from Wem to Wenlock, from Ellesmere to Ironbridge: no town of any great size or consequence, where market days see the cows hugely outnumber the people.

In the non-mobility of the 50's and early 60's, when we had no car to drive and no money to travel very far, I think I developed a clear sense of where we lived. In my mind the borders were defined and well known. I knew what was ours and what was not. On the occasional trip beyond these borders we looked out for the signs, "Welcome To Wales" and looked for them on the way back, "Welcome [Home] To Shropshire. " The county gave us an identity and we identified with it.

So, unsurprisingly, being the greatest of what we had, Shrewsbury was the natural focus, the place you went on special occasions. Moreover, via the Shirehall, it was the town that nurtured and educated me. *Shropshire Education Committee* was stamped on school exercise books and later on grant cheques. When I attended Wellington Grammar School I did not have three lions on my shirt, but I did have the three leopards of the county crest on my blazer.

When it comes to football, then, where else are you going to turn? There's no other league team in the county, so it's an easy choice. You wish Oswestry well and you cheer on Telford at Wembley, but when it comes to it, there's no contest. After all, you want the best!

Besides, like the rest of Shropshire lore (the height of the Wrekin in feet, the date of the world's first iron bridge, Stokesay is a fortified Manor House, the novels of Mary Webb, et cetera.) Shrewsbury Town Football Club, you find, is a part of you and has already permeated your psyche. Either by osmosis, or by viewing the captions below those black and white pictures of the galvanised roof of the Riverside, which appear in the Express & Star, you know them already: Rowley, Pountney, McLaughlin, Clarke. In my young mind they stood alongside Charles Darwin and Lord Clive.

Why not just pick a team that's doing well, or at least has the prospect of doing well? Would you not rather have supported Leeds in the 70's, Liverpool in the 80's and Man U ever since? Chelsea, then – at least they always win the cup? If only it were so simple, but was it not Hamlet who said, "What's Hull to him, or he to Hartlepool?" Perhaps it wasn't, but they're only in Division Three anyway.

But it's not just about results. Results come and go (usually in the 91st minute). We all remember the great wins and the outstanding games, the heroic cup runs and the humbling of our 'betters'. For me though, there's more to it, so many other memorable moments that have little to do with scorelines. Like:

- Mansfield at the Meadow in Sept '69. The fifth home game of the season and goals so far in very short supply. After a frustratingly uneventful second half the ref blows and the players troop off, then, after looking at the clock, the Shrewsbury boys persuade him to restart the game. Back they go for a further frenetic five minutes. Still 0-0, but entertaining in its own way. I know Manchester Utd like to keep on playing if the result's not right, but have they ever stopped and come back on again?
- 1969 was clearly a year of late finishes. Barrow (who?) by November, already miles behind everyone in the table, but ahead early on at the Meadow, where they stayed until the umpteenth minute of second half injury time. Then, at long last, Harkin and ball in the Barrow net, but ref off the pitch into the tunnel. We the crowd (4,002) are left to listen to the results from the whole league read out over the Tannoy. Have you ever watched a game at Anfield and had to wait until ten minutes after the end to know the score? (1-1).
- We all know that footballers have to be in prime physical condition and that the last thing these athletes will consider doing is to abuse their bodies in any way. Okay, a glass of wine with their meal after a game, maybe. Oh, and Bobby Charlton may have smoked ten a day. But did he ever run out towards the Stretford End with a Capstan Full Strength clutched between his teeth? I think not, yet I treasure the memory of Alfie Wood in his pomp during Gregg's Glory Days trotting out of the

tunnel for the warm-up with a ciggie each time. Better still, on one occasion he was joined by Ricky Moir and John Moore. Don't remember the game. Don't remember the score. Doesn't matter.

- Does the score matter? After a season or two, usually not. I remember travelling with my brother to an away game against Port Vale. It was April '71. Town won 1-0, but I don't recall whether Moir blasted one from forty yards, or headed it from two. I remember little of the game except 'the hand of god', or more accurately, the fist of Sandy Brown, rising high above a sea of heads in the Town penalty area to punch the ball away. I can see it now, just as I saw it then, together with the 5,654 other spectators, managers, trainers, twenty two players and subs, tea ladies, turnstile operators, St John's Ambulance men – everyone in the whole of the Five Towns, in fact, except the referee or his linesmen. This was, I recall, something of a disappointment to the Port Vale lads and their fans, but vastly amusing to the travelling troop.
- Not that unwonted items of the anatomy always have such a felicitous role to play. I remember a stirring encounter with Brighton one wintry March night in 1969 when Town were (again) desperate for points to stave off relegation, a fate that was seeming ever more likely as the weeks and points dripped away. After falling behind early in the game (where have I heard that before?), Town strove heroically for the rest of the half and continued to batter Brighton after the break, until at long last they got the equaliser their efforts richly deserved. But, as every follower of football knows, ecstasy is forever (and often all too soon) attended by agony. This night was not to be an exception to that adage. A few moments from time an innocuous Brighton shot strikes Peter Dolby's backside and loops over the helpless Phillips into the Shrewsbury net. Agghhh! The image is as fresh for me today as the air was that night when I stood on the Wakeman End: the ball performing a perfect parabola through the snow-flecked, floodlit night.

As well as agony, however, it's true to say that football has

> more than its share of irony. That game, which ended so full of anguish, was, I believe, the point (no pun, clearly, as there were no points at all that night) at which the season turned towards better things: the infusion of Wood into the front line and the metamorphosis of Trevor Meredith into a midfield dynamo, the Maradona of Division Three.

And many more treasured memories, too numerous to detail.

I was standing on the Riverside one February evening with a few others (13,719) in 1979 for an F.A. Cup replay against Aldershot and overheard someone nearby say it was twenty five years since he'd last been here. How strange, I thought. How could that happen? Had I misheard? Was he talking of something else? Then... twenty something years of my own went by with scarcely an appearance to my name. At least I was no fair-weather fan, I stopped going when they reached the heady heights of the old Division Two.

So it can be done, one can wean oneself away from it, especially if you're living out of the county. Unfortunately, if you fail to get away early enough, if you leave only when your football is fully formed, your escape will never be complete. Season after season you'll know all the players' names and positions, week by week the scores and league placing. There's nothing you can do about that.

Furthermore, when you're away you're an ambassador with a mission to spread the word. Sometime around 1968 I seem to recall the Club employed a company to raise the level of awareness regarding STFC by getting snippets into the national press. In twenty years of teaching in Liverpool schools, during which time I encountered countless thousands of children and hundreds upon hundreds of work colleagues, I believe I did far more to lift the name of Shrewsbury Town into the nation's mind. All of this I did gladly, though pain was often involved, and did for no payment – though, I suppose, I have no firm evidence that a single season ticket sale resulted.

So there you are, like it or loathe it, you're left with it. You may no longer care for the Beatles; you may be seriously contemplating divorce; but when the newspaper comes and the sport page unfolds...

Ups and Downs

"It would be foolish to believe that automatic promotion is automatic in any way whatsoever." – Dave Bassett

Looking at league tables teaches us much about the temporary nature of success in football. Clichés such as "you're only as good as your last result" are magnified by the years. The fortunes of clubs rise and fall, sometimes with alarming alacrity. There are instances of teams that have literally gone from the bottom to the top and back again, Swansea and Northampton being two obvious examples. There are teams that have come from non-league football and done well, at least for a while, before sinking again – such as Hereford, who went from non-league to the old Second Division and back down; Wimbledon actually achieved Premiership status but have slipped out.

There are many clubs that have passed out of the Football League, some into oblivion, others only as far as the Nationwide Conference. Of the teams currently in that league many were formerly in higher pastures within my memory: Barnet, Chester, Doncaster, Hereford, Scarborough and Southport. Dr Martens Premier contains Newport County, whilst the Unibond Premier boasts Accrington, Barrow, Bradford Park Avenue and Gateshead. There are no doubt others lurking somewhere, maybe dreaming of a return to the glory days.

These, as I say, are clubs that I remember in the League and have seen playing at Gay Meadow. To anyone younger several of the names might be strange. Your concept of a club's status depends to a large extent on when you were born or rather when you became conscious of football leagues. Those new to the game might have the idea that Wimbledon "belong" at the highest level and would not associate teams such as Huddersfield, Burnley, Preston, Notts County and Brentford with top division status.

The margin between survival and disaster is a narrow one. This is nicely illustrated by the conflicting fortunes of Brighton and Hereford. After flirting with success at the top level, including the FA Cup Final, Brighton found themselves a few seasons ago staring into the abyss of non-league football or even no football. In a dramatic last game of the season they played and defeated Hereford and in so doing condemned Hereford to expulsion instead. Since that time, whilst Hereford have struggled to impose themselves in the Conference, Brighton have gradually recovered and have just gained their second successive promotion, this time as champions.

These fluctuating fortunes are on one side of the tension that exists within football as in life. They represent competition, the dog-eat-dog half of a delicately balanced equation, with its win-at-all-costs ethos, its tribalistic loyalties and focus on self. Co-operation, the other half of the equation, the opposing force, has several manifestations. On the pitch there is the spirit of fair play – a spirit that transcends even the peace-making rules of the game, that shows itself through handshakes and offers of a hand-up to players on the floor, that causes players to kick the ball out of play (or even catch it instead of shooting, in the case of Paulo Di Canio) when an opponent appears to be seriously injured. In a wider sense there is a network stretching invisibly between clubs, a system of contacts and friendships that brings support, help and advice to other clubs and managers as well as genuine sympathy to the struggling. It is another strand of this side of football – a uniting together in the common good, rather than fighting each other – that Sky Digital currently faces.

Thursday 2nd May, 2002

"Villa will probably play a lot worse than this and lose." – Alan Parry

Aston Villa (home); Malcolm Starkey Testimonial

Previous record in league games:					
Home			Away		
Win	Draw	Lose	Win	Draw	Lose
1	1	1	0	0	3

5-2 (HT 1-1); Rodgers (20 pen, 84), Lowe (52, 57, 90)
Attendance: 2,240
Standpoint: Seat number F183 in the Wakeman Stand, looking over the penalty area at the Wakeman End.

Testimonial games (maybe along with exhibition games, which is a category I've never witnessed) are undoubtedly the least competitive form of spectator football. There is often little in terms of incentive to encourage excellence or even effort. Games played on the training ground have more point, in that performance there might make the difference between being in Saturday's team or not. What testimonial games do offer, however, is a chance for footballers (who as a breed are often characterised as selfish and grasping) to give something. The atmosphere in the ground is also different. Supporters are less critical, less keyed-up, less antagonistic towards the opposition, who have after all agreed to participate out of the goodness of their (or their club's) heart.

How many years do I have to do here before I get a testimonial?

This particular game followed the stereotypical pattern in most respects. There was a more family orientated feel, with parents and grandparents bringing primary age children. The element under-represented in the crowd was youth. There were a few singing on the Riverside, but it is obvious that this age group requires competition in its sport – no adrenalin-rush means no fun.

On the field too things were as one might expect. Villa were very relaxed, being content to show class at times – some of Paul Merson's passing was a magnificent reminder of how great a player he has been (– incidentally it was Merson's performance that drew Peter Dolby's attention in this game: "I didn't realise what a good player he was. He's a McAllister. He has more panache than McAllister."). Lee Hendrie seemed fairly competitive, but generally Villa had nothing to prove. As a result the attacking glory was stolen by Ryan Lowe and Luke Rodgers, Jamie Tolley looked the most effective midfielder on the pitch, and Matt Redmile was a rock in defence.

Incidentally I have seen Paul Merson in a testimonial game at the meadow previously. He was in the Arsenal team that played for Bernard McNally's testimonial in 1988. Frank Worthington scored for the Salop side and I've always thought that would be the basis of a good quiz question. The only other thing I remember about that game was Niall Quinn having a bucket of water thrown over him. Oh, how we laughed.

Salop's selection options for the Villa game had been severely restricted. What with the long-term injuries to Jemson and Jagielka, a recent knee-operation for Ian Dunbavin, the release of Walker, Tretton, Guinan and Rioch because of financial considerations in the light of the ITV Digital situation, and one or two having fled the country, Town were down to the bare bones of a squad. In a laudably magnanimous gesture Gregor Rioch did turn out, and the team performed better as a unit than Villa.

The game was actually quite watchable, the entertainment coming not only from the number of goals but because most of them were high quality. Luke Rodgers hit a penalty after he had been brought down. Lee Hendrie struck an equaliser five minutes later, shooting crisply through a ruck of players following a corner. Shortly after half-time Ryan Lowe smashed a great shot from the edge of the box into the roof of the net. He added to that five minutes later by hitting in the rebound when Luke's shot had found the left goalpost. Villa were right out of it when Luke beat the keeper in a one-on-one, having been released by a through ball from Ryan. Villa did score a goal five minutes later through Steffan Moore, but Ryan Lowe completed a second-half hat-trick when he switched the ball from his left to his right and fired in from inside the box.

I would not want to watch a season of such games, but it was a pleasant way to round off the year – as it was an agreeable occasion for Malcolm Starkey to bring to a close his 40-odd years with the Club.

Soccer Solecisms

"It was not a mistake. It was a blunder." – Gerard Houllier

Colemanballs, gaffes, boobs, talking through the wrong orifice – call them what you will – there's something about football that draws these things out from all those that surround the game more easily (and sometimes more humorously) than sausages are squeezed from a sausage-machine. This "something" seems to inhabit the air around football stadia, inviting syntactical anarchy, turning cliché into a *lingua franca*, sundering language and logic, and encouraging the pompous speech-bubble whilst standing ready to prick it with a pin. The prevalence of this near art form may be due to the fact that football people are so often put in the position where they have to pronounce instantly and authoritatively upon transient events with little time for thought, less time for reflection and with a microphone or two thrust up their nose.

As is apparent, I have celebrated these special *faux pas* here. There are whole books and web-sites dedicated to soccer's wise sayings. Although possibly a peculiarly British phenomenon (and, given M. Cantona's ramblings about sardines and trawlers and the contributions to the art form from other foreigners linked to the English game, I am not sure about that) it has spread beyond these isles. Recently I came across the following in a Norwegian paper:

Historiske perler

«Vel, begge lag kan vinne, eller så kan det bli uavgjort» Ron Atkinson

– As you can see, Big Ron's words reach further than even he might imagine and lose little in the translation.

At the End of the Day

"If you don't believe you can win, there's no point in getting out of bed at the end of the day." – Neville Southall

If statistics are not dear to your heart, skip the next four or so paragraphs.

Before the 2001-2 season Shrewsbury Town had played 2304 League games. We had played these in all Divisions apart from the very top one. On the balance of results we are in debit, winning 792, drawing 630, but losing 882. Likewise the goal tally is not in our favour, being 3093 for, but 3263 against – and I reckon I've seen a fair few of those. Our two best seasons for scoring goals (the only two when we have averaged more than two a game) were two of Arthur Rowley's best: the promotion year of 1958-9, when we scored a century (plus one) for the only time, and the following year. The two worst seasons for scoring goals (each with an average of only 0.87 per game) were the relegation year of 1988-9 and the near-disaster year of 1999-2000. The four seasons with the highest number of points earned per game (all standardised according to the current system of three points to a win) are unsurprisingly the four promotion seasons: 1974-5, 1993-4, 1978-9 and 1958-9. Conversely the five seasons with the lowest number of points per game are, again not surprisingly, the four relegation seasons (1973-4, 1988-9, 1996-7 and 1991-2) and, worst of all, the year of near extinction.

Before the 2001-2 season commenced, of the teams we were scheduled to meet, those we had previously encountered most frequently in the League were Torquay United (24 previous seasons), Mansfield Town (22), Southend United (22), Leyton Orient (20) and Bristol Rovers (20). We had never before played Rushden and Diamonds (apart, that is, from losing in the F.A. Cup). If we ignore the four teams in the Division that Salop have scarcely played because they are not long out of the Conference (Cheltenham, Kidderminster, Macclesfield, and Rushden), we had historically outperformed (in order of our dominance): York City, Oxford United, Swansea City, Halifax Town, Darlington, Lincoln City, Scunthorpe United and Plymouth Argyle. The teams who had historically outperformed Salop (in order of their pre-eminence) are: Luton Town, Southend United, Bristol Rovers, Carlisle United, Leyton Orient, Hull City, Rochdale, Hartlepool, Mansfield Town, Exeter City and Torquay United. This rank order is based on the difference between the respective numbers of victories as a proportion of the number of encounters. Our record of drawing with Halifax (43% of encounters), Plymouth (39%) and Carlisle (38%) is also worth noting.

One conclusion to all the facts of the previous paragraph is that, as history would place at least eleven of the teams ahead of us, Salop has performed relatively well this season. Perhaps it is also interesting to compare one's preconceptions with the facts. Would one automatically believe that Southend, Carlisle and Orient have a superior record against us, or that we have been that much better against York, Oxford and Swansea? Again the changing fortunes of clubs plays a part in our perceptions; it is easy to forget that a team used not to be so successful though it has been in more recent times, and vice versa.

Before I leave the fascinating realm of football statistics I owe it to myself to mention the record of encounters in the league between Shrewsbury Town and Birmingham City. As a teacher in Small Heath I have suffered many a conversation along the lines of: "What team do you support, Sir?" / "Shrewsbury Town." / "Who?" During Salop's time in the old Second Division and into the 1990s such talk was spiced with derisive pre-match comments about what Birmingham City were going to do to Shrewsbury Town. Significantly I rarely heard much about these matches after they had taken place. The following table, I believe, does all the necessary talking.

It has been an interesting year, at times exciting. One might regret not progressing to the play-offs. I don't, in that, although it could be argued that we deserve to be there, I feel we are perhaps not quite ready for promotion and in any case the play-offs are by their nature not only a lottery but stressful. Interestingly Kevin Ratcliffe confessed to being "gutted" after the Luton game, but a couple of weeks on, after having to prune the squad because of lack of ITV Digital money, he was opining that not gaining promotion had been a blessing in disguise. My regrets for the season include the lack of any cup run by Salop, the continued poor quality of refereeing, the slow progress on securing the Club's long-term home, and the part that television and money play in the game. Positives include a much improved performance and team spirit, the development of some promising young players, the way the management has blended this youth with experience and the more stable financial position (television deals notwithstanding).

Football and life go on. However, unless it stays forever in the word-processor, undergoing constant updates and re-writes, the written word cannot keep up. This particular account covers one footballing season but ranges backwards in time over the compass of my life and memory. What it does not aim to do is to look forwards too far. It is thus something of an unfinished symphony. A plethora of unanswered questions hang in the air, some of which will already be answered before you are reading this, others may yet be scarcely formed. Some of those it is possible to state now include:

Salop's record in league games versus Birmingham City:					
Home			Away		
Win	Draw	Lose	Win	Draw	Lose
5	3	1	4	2	3

Which clubs will be the winners and losers when all the leagues and cup competitions are played out for the season?

What will be the outcome of the ITV Digital débâcle?

How many clubs will fold?

How many metatarsals will not make it through the World Cup tournament?

Will England win the World Cup?

Will Third Division defences learn to cope with Luke Rodgers?

How long will the aforementioned small player remain with Salop?

Will he be the first Salop player to be sold for over a million?

Will Salop win promotion as champions in 2003?
When will the New Meadow become a reality?
What happened to the band?
What does “harka” really mean?
Will professional football as we know it still exist in Britain in ten years’ time?

However the future resolves itself, let us keep that Latin tag (or is it a prayer?) always to heart….
Floreat Salopia.

Christmas Crossword Solution

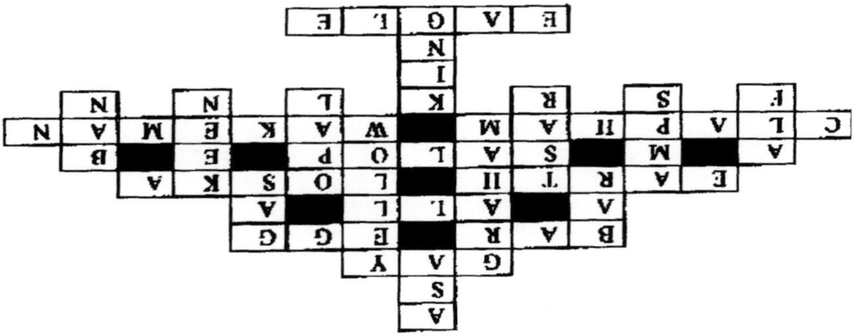

Party Game Solution

There are of course no correct answers. You may, however, if the pubs are shut and there's nothing on the tele, extend the game by adding further suitable names and resolutions for friends to pair up. – Hours of harmless fun for all.

If you have enjoyed this book you may like the following works of fiction:

The story of a disastrous school re-union. Probably the first, and possibly the last, novel to contain a gratuitous and completely irrelevant reference to *A Large Scotch*.

Festival concerns the activities of a group of students, one of whose major preoccupation is putting on comedy revues. Like all with similar ambitions they end up on the Edinburgh Fringe, but on their way pass through Shropshire. The novel almost certainly contains more references to Shrewsbury Town than any previously published – but it does not mention coracles (I promise).